WELCOME 2 HOUSTON

AFRICAN AMERICAN MUSIC IN GLOBAL PERSPECTIVE

Portia K. Maultsby, Series Editor
Archives of African American Music and Culture
Indiana University

A list of books in the series appears at the end of this book.

WELCOME 2 HOUSTON

HIP HOP HERITAGE
IN HUSTLE TOWN

LANGSTON COLLIN WILKINS

UNIVERSITY OF ILLINOIS PRESS
Urbana, Chicago, and Springfield

Publication of this book was supported in part by a grant from the Judith McCulloh Endowment for American Music.

Library of Congress Cataloging-in-Publication Data
Names: Wilkins, Langston Collin, author.
Title: Welcome 2 Houston: hip hop heritage in Hustle Town /
    Langston Collin Wilkins.
Other titles: Welcome to Houston
Description: Urbana: University of Illinois Press, 2023. | Series:
    African American music in global perspective | Includes
    bibliographical references and index.
Identifiers: LCCN 2022049648 (print) | LCCN 2022049649 (ebook)
    | ISBN 9780252045158 (hardback) | ISBN 9780252087295
    (paperback) | ISBN 9780252054525 (ebook)
Subjects: LCSH: Rap (Music)—Texas—Houston—History and
    criticism. | Hip-hop—Texas—Houston—History. | African
    Americans—Texas—Houston—Social life and customs. |
    Automobiles—Customizing—Texas—Houston. | Chopped
    and screwed (Music)—History and criticism.
Classification: LCC ML3531.W548 2023 (print) | LCC ML3531 (ebook)
    | DDC 782.42164909764/1411—dc23/eng/20221014
LC record available at https://lccn.loc.gov/2022049648
LC ebook record available at https://lccn.loc.gov/2022049649

contents

ACKNOWLEDGMENTS

This project started well before I entered the field in 2011. It began over twenty-five years ago, in 1996, when I was given my first hip hop record—the Geto Boys' *The Resurrection* (1996). That album changed my life. It tuned my ears to the complicated world around me and sparked an unrelenting love for hip hop music and culture. I would not have purchased that album on my own. Yes, my father made me a hip hop fan. My love for Black music, literature, and politics comes from him. My father had keen insight into who I was and who I would become. When he spoke, I listened. He never steered me wrong. He was a writer, and I wish he was here to see this book on a shelf. I find a small amount of comfort knowing that he's up there, above the clouds, looking down on me with pride.

I also want to thank Christina Harrison-Wilkins, Yolanda Wilkins, Arielle Wilkins, and the rest of my family for your unwavering support. You all nourished my hip hop obsession, gifting records, listening to my hip hop chatter when no one else would, and encouraging my random idea to study hip hop culture in graduate school. You helped me indulge my interests without fear. I cannot adequately articulate how much you mean to me.

Thank you to Dr. Portia Maultsby and Dr. Fernando Orejuela. While your contributions to this book are both incalculable and invaluable, I want even more to thank you for the guidance you provided throughout my career. Through your mentorship, I slowly but surely learned not only the field of ethnomusicology, but also what it means to be a strong, confident, and intellectually rigorous scholar. I could not have reached this point without your help, and for that, I cannot thank you enough.

Thank you to the Houston Museum of African American Culture (HMAAC) and the Folklife and Traditional Arts Department of the Houston Arts Alliance (HAA) for providing financial support during my time in the field, and also for allowing me to develop my fieldwork and public programming skills. I want to especially shout out HMAAC CEO John Guess and former HAA folklorist Pat Jasper. The Houston Slab Parade is the greatest achievement of my career and I sincerely thank you for believing in that project.

I must thank my village of friends who helped me navigate graduate school, professional life, and this project. These friends include, but are not limited to: Levon Williams, Robert "Deejay" Jordan, Jeff Barrows, Fredara Hadley, Rafi Hasan, Nicholas Battle, Mike Lee, Thomas Richardson, Raynetta Wiggins, Timon Kaple, Nate Gibson, Lindsay Richman, Arnald Beckwith, Bradley Hanson, Eric Harvey, Tricia Ferdinand, Sarah Farmer, June Evans, Kate Aguilar, James Webb-Glass, David Lehman, and Quan Ngo. I am grateful to you all.

Major thank you to my Phi Beta Sigma Fraternity brothers, too. I sincerely appreciate your support. GOMAB!

I want to give a quick shout out to Donnie Houston, Lance Scott Walker, John Nova Lomax, Rocky Rockett, Julie Grob, Shelby Stewart, Maco Faniel, and all of the good folks who are working hard to preserve and celebrate Houston's music culture.

Finally, I want to thank all the Houston hip hoppers for their contributions to this project. That includes Andre "007" Barnes, The Aspiring Me, B.G., Big Love, Big Pokey, Bishop Black, the Bloc Boyz Click, China Boy, Cl'Che, Corey Paul, Craig "BBC" Long, The Mighty D-Risha, DJ Chill, Doughbeezy, EDF, E.S.G., Ganxsta NIP, Icey Hott, Justice Allah, Lil Randy, Lil Raskull, Meyagi, Nasty Nique Roots, OG Scott, P Izm the Mack, Flat Pat/Purple Bastard, Rob Gullatte, Sketch the Journalist, Tre-9, Von Won, and Zavey. Thank you for offering me, a relative stranger, access to your private thoughts about art and life. I admire and feel a sense of kinship with you all. I hope this book represents you well.

INTRODUCTION

"Honestly, if I wasn't from Houston, I wouldn't know what to do musically," says Earsell Fitzgerald casually, leaning his large frame over the small table to emphasize his point (EDF, interview with the author, 2012). "I just feel that my city's heritage and history is a whole lot more valuable than people give it credit for." We are together at Whole Foods, one of the many random places around the city of Houston that hosted my interviews for this project. It is an uncharacteristically mild summer day in Houston, and Earsell is wearing a button-down Oxford shirt and khaki pants, the modest uniform that he wears during his day job in IT. At night, Earsell transforms into rapper EDF, eschewing the IT wear for fly sneakers, jeans, designer T-shirts, and baseball caps.

For EDF hip hop music is a grammar rooted in the particulars of local experience. You can enjoy the art and decipher meanings on a surface level, but you cannot truly understand the music if you are not from its place of origin. "I can recite every Jay-Z song, but I can't relate to Jay because he is from New York. They hustle different and live by a different code of ethics," he tells me. "But, if you put on a Scarface or Geto Boys CD or Fat Pat, who's one of my greatest influences, I'm going to understand it" (EDF, interview with the author, 2012).

EDF could add archivist to his list of occupations since his music, both organically and intentionally, preserves local hip hop heritage. EDF's slow, syrupy flow and stellar charisma is reminiscent of late Houston rap luminary Fat Pat. Lyrically, EDF creates an aspirational plane that's situated in the nexus between street life and nightlife. He typically rhymes over beats that are downtempo and atmospheric, yet "bop" at the same time. It is even in his name, as EDF is an homage to E.S.G., another Houston-area legend and member of the Screwed Up Click.

In that moment, on that uncharacteristically mild afternoon in summertime Houston, we were two culture workers coming together to discuss the hip hop heritage that we so dearly treasured. Our meeting that afternoon was charged with an intense pride of place that gave birth to an impenetrable love for local hip hop sound, style, and life.

It turns out that our shared interest in Houston hip hop was not the only thing EDF and I had in common. We both grew up in Hiram Clarke, a predominately African American working-class neighborhood in south central Houston. It is a quaint and charming neighborhood nestled where the behemoth Harris County touches neighboring Ft. Bend County. The neighborhood has the peculiar distinction of being simultaneously remote and convenient. It is a mere fifteen minutes away from important local institutions such as the Medical Center, the Zoo, and Reliant Stadium, the home of the NFL's Houston Texans. However, at the same time, State Road 90 acts as a physical and symbolic barrier between the neighborhood and these mainstream institutions. This sense of disconnection is exacerbated by the neighborhood's positioning outside of the 610 Loop, the state highway system that forms a circular boundary around the city's central residential and business areas. The neighborhood's boundaries are actively negotiated and policed by its resident base and are therefore constantly in flux. However, most would agree that State Highway 90, West Fuqua St., and its namesake Hiram Clarke Blvd. form a border of sorts.

Within these constantly influx boundaries, the predominantly African American residency can be seen partaking in iconic features of your typical American neighborhood. From a socioeconomic standpoint, the area vacillates between the upper reaches of the poor and working classes and the lower middle class. These residents typically inhabit brick, ranch-style homes with two-car garages that sit on large patches of fenced land. Families shop for groceries at Foodarama, a small, dimly lit chain that anchors a modest strip center on West Fuqua St. Alternatively, families go to Fiesta, a location of the Texas-based chain that rests on the corner of South Main and South

Post Oak, a major thoroughfare. Most of the neighborhood kids move from Hobby Elementary to Dick Dowling Middle School to Madison High School. On Saturday night, adults hang out at nightclubs like Club Manhattan or the Red Rooster, or informal social spaces such as Waddell's Food Store on the corner of White Heather and West Orem. On Sunday morning, residents have their pick of churches, from the small, like Hiram Clarke Missionary Baptist Church, to the large, like Brentwood Baptist Church, which serves over five thousand residents, including many celebrities.

Hiram Clarke's sense of inner-city suburbia is disrupted by multi-dimensional effects of racial segregation and economic inequality. At the entrance to the neighborhood, visitors are greeted by a sign reading "Welcome to Hiram Clarke" that is surrounded by several working-age Black men perched on upside-down milk crates, drinking beer to make the day go by faster. It is a place where solidly middle-class homeowners can live next door to renters who struggle to keep the lights on. While many youths overcome the neighborhood's underfunded educational institutions to graduate high school and make it to college, there are many others who succumb to the effects of educational inequality and drop out of school. The crime rate is higher than average. Therefore the police are a constant presence, whether on the ground in cars or flying overhead in helicopters.

Territorial identity is an important social process within Houston's Black neighborhoods. I understood this to some extent since birth, but it became much more explicit when I matriculated to Westbury High School, which was situated in a neighborhood area of the same name. Most of Westbury's student body lived in the working-class to lower-middle-class neighborhoods that fed into the school, and the characteristics of these neighborhoods became associated with students' public identity. Roaming the halls, students shouted out the names of streets like West Airport and neighborhoods like Fondren Southwest. Students expressed pride in "the West," the collective identity of all the Black southwestern Houston neighborhoods, for which calls, hand signs, and T-shirts developed.

For Black Houstonians, this pride of place can extend beyond high school and into adulthoods that take you into different physical areas and shifting cultural contexts. If you live in these areas, you understand that the neighborhood is part of your intellectual and emotional makeup. Everything you do in this world, in this sense, reflects the collection of streets, institutions, and people that raised you. When I asked him whether he felt Hiram Clarke was part of his personal identity, EDF offered a passionate explanation:

> It depends on how true you are to yourself. My co-workers in corporate America ask me "Where are you from?" I proudly tell them, "I'm from Hiram Clarke, Texas." I'm currently living in Pearland now and it's a blessing. But, I'm from Hiram Clarke, Texas, the Southside. Your 'hood is only as popular as you. If you choose to be a goon, and go swanga shopping every night, and you get arrested and you're in county [jail], that's all niggas ask about in jail, "Where you from?" That's all they care about. (Interview with the author, 2012)

Black Houstonians come to embody their 'hoods on various levels, and the 'hoods become inscribed in your personal and cultural practices. This is very much evident in Houston-based hip hop music. Place is central in the music of Houston artists such as Scarface and Paul Wall, who ground local concerns in their lyrics and perform primarily for local and regional audiences. I often heard shout outs to Houston streets, neighborhoods, and the city itself on their Houston-based recordings. Eventually, I began to understand that these artists constructed their identities around markers associated with various spaces and places. Similar to my classmates, they believe that where you are from says much about who you are (or should be). Thus, place was a marker of identity. My personal experiences in the city and my long-term engagement with the music inspired my interest in examining territorial expressions in Houston-based hip hop music.

Constructing identities in association with place, place-based markers, and other territorial expressions is not unique to the Houston hip hop scene, of course. Artists have exhibited strong identification with geographic areas since the dawn of hip hop culture. Within the early graffiti scene in New York City, a writer's tag included his or her nickname along with street number. Subway cars became the most valued canvas for graffiti artists because the cars travel throughout the city, spreading these alias-signature pieces to neighboring areas. Geography was an instrumental factor in two of the most infamous conflicts in hip hop history: the MC Shan/KRS-One battle and the East-Coast/West Coast beef. The mid-1980s conflict between Queens-based MC Shan and Bronx-based KRS-One stemmed from an assumed confusion over which borough created hip hop and whose scene was the most spectacular. The same can be said of the mid-1990s conflict between California transplant Tupac Shakur and New York City's Notorious B.I.G. The tension between the two men triggered a war between artists from the East Coast and West Coast as fellow artists chose to take place-determined sides. Even today, when hip hop has become a trans-national industry, the most popular rap artists are identified with their home places. Jay-Z is perceived as a manifestation of New York hip hop and cosmopolitanism, and he has reinforced this through songs such as the immensely popular "Empire State of Mind" (2009). T.I.'s popularity is tied to his ability to creatively express the particularities of the Atlanta drug scene. Since 2012, rapper Kendrick Lamar has represented himself as a child of post–LA riots Compton, California. In short, place, in its various forms, has historically been an essential component in the construction of hip hop identity on all levels.

Compared to that of other locales, Houston hip hop has a unique and pervasive identity that has been passed down from one micro-generation to another. The sound, style, and way of life has persisted despite shifts within the larger national hip hop and popular music landscapes that have undermined other local scenes. This book critically explores this phenomenon through case studies that analyze the complex relationships among place, identity, music, and heritage within Houston's hip hop music scene. In Houston, hip hop heritage functions as a creative manifestation of Black locals' embodiment of place. More explicitly, Houston hip hop heritage is a communicative medium through which artists and audiences negotiate, celebrate, and capitalize on their complex relationship with place. This process can be traced through various segments of the scene, from the more street-based artist to avant-garde underground rappers to Christian hip hop artists. It can also be seen within the local, hip hop–related vernacular car culture called slab. Within each of these segments, streets, apartment buildings, neighborhoods, and the city itself are cultural resources that locals employ in a wide variety of ways. Ultimately, I explore how the interaction between people, music, and place created a cultural heritage that artists negotiate, voluntarily or not, in a myriad of ways.

This book is based on fieldwork that I conducted in Houston, Texas, over the course of several years, with the biggest chunk between September 2011 and August 2012. During this time, I resided in my parents' home in the Hiram Clarke neighborhood, which happens to have a very important hip hop legacy in the city. Many local rappers such as Big Mello, Big Steve, Icey Hott of Street Military, EDF, and Mr. 3–2 were raised in the neighborhood. Hiram Clarke is also the second home of Screwed Up Records & Tapes, the hip hop record store opened by local luminary DJ Screw. The store was originally located in the South Park neighborhood but relocated to Hiram Clarke in February of 2012. Living in Hiram Clarke offered the opportunity for ongoing engagement with Houston's local hip hop culture as well as the larger African American Houston culture that gave birth to this tradition.

Much of my data comes from interviews that I conducted with more than twenty-five local rap artists, producers, and managers. The traditional demographics of this group were overwhelmingly African American and male, reflecting the general characteristics of the scene. Women were very active on the business side of the scene during my time in the field. I engaged with many female managers, publicists, and club promoters, but I did not see many female rap artists in the spaces I engaged. In their excellent study of female rappers in Detroit, Rebekah Farrugia and Kellie D. Hay note that "women in hip hop face a double layer of misogyny, one that comes from the extreme local and the other emanating from the commercial music industry and the patriarchal conditions in which these spaces are steeped" (Farrugia and Hay 2017, 66). I suspect that Houston's hip hop scene reflects the same gender dynamics. I interviewed female rapper Cl'Che, of the Screwed Up Click and South Park Coalition, after meeting her following one of her performances. Contrary to my male informants, Cl'Che preferred to be interviewed over the phone. I do not know why she preferred a remote interview, but I can imagine that physical distance can be a protective measure as female artists navigate the male-dominated hip hop scene. It is a reminder that the view of space (and construction of space) of one who is not a cisgendered man can be very different from that of cisgendered men. Lacking time and access, I struggled to get the perspective of female emcees within the scene. This is unfortunate because the intersection of their race and gender gives them unique perspectives that would further enrich this study.

The ages of my interviewees varied, and they represented hip hoppers who contributed to different phases of Houston hip hop's development. The first group includes artists who began recording during the developmental period of the Houston hip hop scene, from the late 1980s through the early 1990s. The second group is composed of artists who initiated the process of localization through their recordings from the mid-1990s through the middle of the next decade. The third group features up-and-coming artists who began recording around 2005 to 2010, as the local screwed-and-chopped sound began hitting the national landscape.

My personal connections to the city of Houston and Houston hip hop culture were useful in establishing relationships with participants in the scene. I contacted most of my interviewees through email, making sure to mention that I grew up in Hiram Clarke and other parts of the Southside. I feel that this worked to exhibit my cultural competency and bolster my cultural capital. I think my status as a graduate student was influential as well. Many artists seemed proud that someone raised in their environment could attain such educational achievements. Most artists accepted my interview requests in informal fashion.

In many instances, artists suggested possible locations for interviews, often without giving explicit directions or information about the locations. I think they assumed that since I grew up in Houston, I would readily know the location of these places. That was true for most cases. For example, rapper Ganxsta NIP suggested that we meet at a Walgreens drug store on the corner of West Belfort and Fondren in Southwest Houston. This particular Walgreens location happened to be only a few miles from my former high school and was therefore a place I had frequented over the years. Big Pokey of the Screwed Up Click told me to meet him at Yates High School in Third Ward, which is a neighborhood with which I am intimately familiar. I picked rapper/producer Icey Hott up from his house in Northside's Settegast neighborhood and drove him to Greenspoint Mall, where we conducted the interview at the legendary Music Depot record store. I was, to some extent, a cultural insider who held experiential knowledge of spaces and places important to these artists.

Despite my cultural competency and relatability, participants' general openness really surprised me. They seemed very willing to share information that ranged from the deeply personal to the highly sensitive. Also, on several occasions, participants openly consumed drugs such as marijuana and lean in front of me. During one memorable interview, an artist and several of his friends passed around and consumed various drugs under a carport that was clearly visible to neighboring homes and passersby. While studying the slab scene one night, a slab rider allowed me to photograph the inside of his car. While doing so, I noticed what appeared to be an assault rifle—an AK-47—resting on the passenger seat. I was taken aback, not out of fright or nervousness, but simply because this person so willingly let a stranger into his vehicle knowing that a likely loaded gun was in plain sight. Houston hip hoppers exhibited an unforeseen level of openness and trust, which afforded me a rich and edifying field experience.

I must note that as I immersed myself in the Houston hip hop scene, I established close personal relationships that helped me immensely. Artists such as Bishop Black, Icey Hott, That Purple Bastard, Nasty Nique, and the Bloc Boyz Click became personal confidants who helped me navigate the scene's complex landscape. Relatedly, I felt reciprocity was important. I understood that these individuals were giving me their time, knowledge, and experience, so I made it a point to be helpful to them wherever I could. For example, I wrote a biography for the Mighty D-Risha, an underground rapper. I built and continue to manage Icey Hott's artist website. My social media pages became a promotional space for the many local hip hop artists that I interacted with. For me, fieldwork went beyond research. It facilitated the development of genuine friendships and allowed me to contribute to the city and scene that has long meant so much to me.

HOUSTON HIP HOP as HeRITaGe

Defining *heritage* has been a contested terrain, with approaches readily shifting in accordance with sociopolitical concerns around the globe. The term's democratic evolution is, in some ways, a good thing, as such concepts should be a bit malleable, reflecting new and more accessible ways of thinking. However, this constant rendering has led to a field of definitions of *heritage* that is either too open or too limiting according to different critics. As Les Roberts (2014) writes, "heritage marshals a jumble of overlapping, disparate and, at times, contradictory meanings that accommodate a burgeoning array of perspectives that frustrate attempts to pin the concept down."

Andy Bennett (2015) synthesizes common definitions of *heritage* when defining it as the "specific canonical representations of custom, tradition, and place that are presented as an integral part of collective identity in particular regional and national contexts" (19). Other scholars add to this definition of *heritage* by pointing to its temporality. Barbara Kirshenblatt-Gimblett (1995) has succinctly called heritage "a mode of cultural production in the present that has recourses to the past" (369). Les Roberts (2014) writes that "cultural heritage is better understood as a process, in that its meanings and uses are socially, spatially and temporally enacted, and, as such, are constantly being remade and negotiated" (6).

Of course, discussions of heritage cannot avoid engaging the 2003 UNESCO Convention for Safeguarding Intangible Cultural Heritage and its resulting paradigm. Officially enacted in 2006, the treaty was intended to offer guidance and direction for nation-states and territories looking to recognize and protect the aspects of culture that weren't physical and permanent like monuments, sites, and such. UNESCO'S intangible cultural heritage (ICH) list is broken down into several genres or what they call "domains":

    a. oral traditions and expressions
    b. performing arts
    c. social practices, rituals, and festive events
    d. knowledge and practices concerning nature and the universe
    e. traditional craftsmanship

Performing arts, like the other domains, can be further broken down into several subdomains including music. Music, in fact, dominates the ICH list. As de-Miguel-Molina and Boix-Domenech note, music accounts for over 50% of the registered entries as of 2018 (de-Miguel-Molina and Boix-Domenech 2021, 3). This includes globally recognized sounds like Jamaican reggae and Spanish flamenco but also deeply regional styles like the Klapa singing tradition of southern Croatia and Indian Sakirtana ritual singing.

Hip Hop has not been readily understood as heritage even though its constitution reflects the powerful intersections of place, identity, and performance. I posit that this has been the case for multiple reasons. First, the lack of hip hop heritization is a biproduct of popular music's contested status in the heritage landscape. Conventional definitions of heritage have historically made little space for popular music forms. The mass-produced, mass-marketed, and trans-local nature of perceived popular music forms runs counter to the unofficial attributes of heritage forms (Bennett 2015, 18). For people who adhere to this idea, popular music lacks genuine connection to identifiable and bonded communities. It is too widely disseminated, far too rooted in the capitalist-focused commercial music industry, and ultimately too accessible. It lacks authenticity, that intangible and immeasurable quality that unproductively complicates discourse about so many cultural practices. Of course, there are outliers like the case of blues in Chicago and Mississippi and the burgeoning "heritage rock" field, but by and large, popular music occupies a precarious place in heritage discourse.

Hip hop's presence within the commercial music industry obfuscates its roots in local lived experience. As I show throughout this book, hip hop is the everyday social activity of Black communities crystalized into an intangible creative product. Hip hop artists index the experiences, practices, and values of bounded communities, imagining them into culturally specific rhymes laid over beats tuned to local ears. Even globally relevant hip hop styles were born out of these hyperlocal relationships. Further exacerbating matters is the impact of recent technology on the once prominent territoriality in hip hop culture. Web 2.0 has largely eroded the sense of regional identity within the hip hop musical landscape. The spatial boundaries that once policed artists' stylistic choices have been dissolved. Regional styles continue to persist, but they are now being openly adopted by artists from outside their places of origin. Nevertheless, no matter how widely it travels or what method it used to get there, hip hop remains grounded in local realities.

Houston's hip hop scene is composed of a variety of participants who operate around a sense of collective heritage that derives from their place-bound experience. The heritage has a core set of identity markers that, as I will later discuss, emerged directly out of local "street culture." Screw music is the hallmark of local hip hop heritage. The term refers to both a remixing technique and a production style and has its origins in a deejaying technique developed by DJ Screw known as "screwed and chopped." The first part of the technique, "screwing," involves the use of a turntable or other device to slow the tempo of a record. Chopping results from the use of two copies of the same record, with the second copy playing a beat behind the first. DJs then crossfade the mixer to shift between the two tracks, creating a doubling effect half a second apart. Chops are essentially repeated phrases used in a rhythmic fashion. As a production style, the aesthetic of screw music derives from the sound of DJ Screw's mixtapes. Screw-based instrumentals feature slower tempos ranging between 60–70 beats per minute (Petrusich 2014). These tempos are much slower than the music produced in other southern centers such as Atlanta and New Orleans, which can be between 100 and

140 bpms. In addition to the slowed tempos, screwed music features rich extended basslines and ambient sounds that create a psychedelic and atmospheric brand of hip hop music.

Houston's hip hop heritage also includes two sociomusical practices that are both independent traditions but are also inextricably tied to the musical form: slabs and lean. *Slab* refers to the unique urban car culture that developed in Houston's Black neighborhoods in the early 1980s. Slabs are not only commonplace in lyrics. The cars are prominently featured in local music videos as well as depicted on local hip hop–related fashions and images. Also known as syrup, barre, or oil, lean is a drug concoction composed of codeine-based cough syrup mixed with soda or liquor. Similar to slabs, lean is popular subject matter within local hip hop lyrics and regularly referenced on album covers, in advertisements, and in music videos.

This book examines Houston hip hop heritage as a social process rooted in people's connection to place. The heritage was born out of and continues to be sustained by Houstonians' deep bonds with the various spaces and places that constitute their understandings of the city. Streets, apartment buildings, neighborhoods, and other places operate as cultural capital that is inherited and then embodied. This embodied place is commonly articulated through social activity and directly influenced the emergence of screw, slabs, and lean as individual practices and an identifiable cultural heritage. In Houston, many local artists actively safeguard this heritage through their music, both organically and intentionally. This community of artists deeply embraces the screw sound and related practices to express their deep local pride. They occupy a relatively privileged place among a local audience that shares their pride of place.

In common discourse, heritage is understood as a virtuous practice—a way to build and affirm local community through the preservation of history and propagation of local identity. However, heritage is a complicated process that can be as reductive or limiting as it is empowering. Hip hop culture is a tradition whose foundational elements (emceeing, deejaying, b-boying, and graffiti) have been consistent across African diasporic time and space. But, at least musically, hip hop has also been about innovation and personalization. Practitioners mold the sound to fit their contexts and creative impulses, both individual and communal. To that end, a dominant local hip hop heritage can become a hegemonic weight that suppresses idiosyncratic innovation and marginalizes seemingly oppositional musical identities. I explore this phenomenon through a stylistically and culturally diverse set of artists, sometimes called underground or alternative, whose styles negotiate local heritage and the desire for free expression and local relevance.

Screw's position as heritage is further complicated by the fact that its core elements emerged out of Houston street life and, to this point, it continues to reflect those realities to varying degrees. Lyrical themes within the music, the materialism of slab, and lean in general can stand in stark contrast to people's ways of life. This can be true for a number of underground artists, but it is also true for members of the city's culturally significant Christian hip hop community. One would think that these artists would avoid the screw heritage at all costs as it seemingly opposes their ministerial concerns. However, it is quite the opposite as local Christian artists carefully and strategically pull from the screw tradition to connect with potential disciples for whom the music reflects their spatially informed lived experience.

Theorizing Space and Place

The concepts of space and place undergird this study. Therefore, it is important to both define the two concepts and discuss the relationship between them at this early point. Numerous scholars have offered multi-faceted conceptions of space. Central to this study, however, is philosopher and sociologist Henri Lefebvre's (1991) concept of "social space," a complex social product that he defines as "part of an interaction between subjects and their surroundings" (17). Geographer Doreen Massey expounds on Lefebvre's definition noting that "social space consists of all of the network and complexities of social interaction and interconnections, whether they be small scale or global in their reach" (Massey 1995, 54). Social space is generated by three separate but interacting spatial entities: conceived space, lived space, and perceived space. The first, "conceived space," includes the ideas, knowledge, plans, codes, and memories that shape and regulate social space (Van Igen 2003, 202). As part of conceived space, government officials, city planners, architects, and others with culturally defined power use discursive activity to impose order and control within a space. "Lived space" functions in the experiential realm and relates to the symbolic meanings attached to space by its inhabitants. This includes signs, structures, murals, and other elements that can articulate the meaning or value attached to a space for its inhabitants.

The third part of this triad, "perceived space," can also be called "place" (Agnew 2011, 324) and includes material or physical sites within spaces such as streets, corners, stores, houses, neighborhoods, and cities. It also refers to the sites and social activities that make up our daily routines or everyday life. Places are the tangible, particular nodes within social space. As Massey further notes, "a place is formed out of the particular set of social relations which inter[sect] at any particular point" (Massey 1995, 168). Places are where the material flows of space become concrete and are able to be geographically located, physically entered, experienced, felt, and identified through labeling or naming. Geographer John Agnew synthesizes the relationship between space and place and explains that "places are woven together through space by movement and the network ties that produce places as changing constellations of human commitments, capacities, and strategies" (Agnew 2011, 325). In other words, space is an abstract and fluid boundary that includes the practices, knowledge, codes, rules, meanings, and relationships that impact individuals as they move through a network of places (or physical space) in the course of their daily routines.

For instance, a sacred place within the city can be a church, mosque, synagogue, or similar spiritual site. A network of such sites, along with various religious communities, teachings, religious art, and local zoning laws that affect religious land use may comprise "sacred space" within a city. Likewise educational space within a city contains school buildings, the student population, and the various educations and requirements that shape activities and behaviors in the school buildings. Hip hop scholar Murray Forman succinctly summarizes the relationship between spaces and places. For Forman place "defines the immediate locale of human intervention in the particular, whereas space is the expanse of mobile trajectories through which subjects pass in their circulation between or among distinct and varied places" (Forman 2002, 25).

The space of the local hip hop scene—places of production, performance, and engagement—is of prime importance to this book. The hip hop scene includes many places such as bars, nightclubs, recording studios, radio stations, and recording labels scattered throughout the city. Locally produced hip hop music, naturally, is the primary element of the lived realm. The music gives the scene its concrete function and purpose. However, the entire scene is driven, in the conceived realm, by a strong cultural identity. The aesthetic composition of the music, as well as the particular sites that define the scene, are informed by the extent to which artists embrace local hip hop heritage. This book is an ethnographic look at how the relationship between spatial practices, identity, and musical performances produces Houston's hip hop heritage.

THE HOUSTON HIP HOP SCENE: AN OVERVIEW

Houston's hip hop scene is part of a regional hip hop continuum that some call the "Dirty South." Along with Houston, the "Dirty South" includes popular regional rap scenes in New Orleans, Atlanta, Memphis, and Miami among others. The term was coined by Atlanta-based rapper Cool Breeze and has been used to identify both a larger regional Southern rap identity and the impact that the region has had on the national hip hop landscape. The hip hop industry had long been dominated by sounds emanating out of New York and California. The rise of the Dirty South in the late 1990s helped diversify approaches to music making and perspectives on Black life within hip hop culture both national and globally.

I personally have complicated feelings about the term "Dirty South." While there are shared aesthetic approaches to music making among Southern rap scenes, synthesizing them into a single brand tends to obscure unique local traditions and music experiences. Southern hip hop artists have embraced the term to various degrees, but more than that they seek to highlight hyperlocal identities and experience. Hip hop has traditionally been competitively territorial, and that remains true in the South. For example, local rapper Dunta resolutely defends the uniqueness of Houston's hip hop heritage: "We're totally different down here in Houston. Our style ain't the same as nobody's. Everybody else has something in common, but not Houston. We got a totally different swag as everyone else. We got our own thang. We got our own drugs. So yea, we ain't like no one else" (interview with the author, 2012). In addition, in both academic and popular discourse, the term "Dirty South" has been largely informed by the Atlanta hip hop scene, a cultural and commercial behemoth. Atlanta's cultural and music industry dynamics do not absolutely reflect that of other scenes. In short, in its execution, "Dirty

South" undermines powerful regional nuance within Southern hip hop as well as artists' and audiences' intense desire for singularity.

Regina Bradley's (2021) recent "hip hop south" framework offers an alternative and more productive approach to understanding the Southern hip hop experiences. Bradley's "hip hop South" centers on "the experiences of black southerners who came of age in the 1980s and 1990s and use hip-hop culture to buffer themselves from the historical narrative and expectations of civil rights movement era blacks and their predecessors" (Bradley 2021, 6). The hip hop South dismantles romantic and reductive notions of Southern life, preferring to combine "cornerstones of the past using hip-hop to carve out a space where the complexity of experiences in the post–civil rights era can breathe" (Bradley 2021, 6). "Hip hop South" creates space for the multitude of unique Black experiences in the South and the locally specific hip hop sounds produced across the region.

The Houston hip hop scene is a multi-faceted scene that features a diverse collective of artists. In this study, I identify three different artistic communities operating within the scene. I call the first community "street-based artists." Sonically, their musical preference is the screw sound and their lyrics commonly feature references to slabs, syrup, and other street-based practices. The second collective is made up of the "underground hip hop artists." These are artists and fans who identify with the styles that emerged outside of Houston, especially those identified as underground. While this group embraces the local hip hop scene, they do not want to be limited by this identity. The final group is "Christian hip hop artists," who use hip hop as a vehicle for communicating the Christian message.

Houston hip hop artists have traditionally operated outside of the mainstream recording industry, preferring to record and release music through locally based independent companies. Rap-A-Lot Records has long been the premier independent label in the city and has released albums by legendary Houston artists including the Geto Boys, Devin the Dude, Pimp C, and Z-Ro. Swishahouse, formed in the late 1990s by deejays Michael Watts and OG Ron C, has also been a formidable indie label, releasing albums by Slim Thug, Paul Wall, and Grammy award–winning Chamillionaire. Houston's indie labels have been able to achieve much success by partnering with regional distributors that place their music in mom-and-pop stores and major retailers across the south. Recently, keeping with national trends, Houston artists have eschewed record labels altogether, releasing music through internet spaces such as Bandcamp, Datpiff for mixtapes, or streaming sites like Spotify, Apple Music, and Tidal.

Houston hip hop artists perform live as much as possible. During my time in the field, multiple rap shows took place on any given night. Most of these performances took place in small neighborhood clubs and after-hours spots such as S & S Sports Bar in the Southside and JJs Sports Bar on the Northside. Downtown Houston was a prime area for hip hop performances via clubs Jet Lounge, Toc Bar, and Notsuoh. These shows most often featured a single headliner, supported by three to four opening acts. Showcases, however, have also become popular. These shows feature between ten and twenty up-and-coming acts that perform no more than three songs each. Block parties occur monthly throughout the summer and are similar to showcases, but typically feature more established artists.

While a long-standing and relatively large scene, Houston hip hop has lacked consistent media coverage and promotion. Until the recent emergence of IheartMedia-owned 93.7 The Beat, Radio One's 97.9 KBXX (The Boxx) was the city's only hip hop–oriented traditional radio station. It continues to be the most popular and culturally resonant hip hop station. Although it does live broadcasts from local events and features shows by prominent local deejays, the station has been criticized for not supporting local artists. Justice Allah synthesizes KBXX criticisms in the following comment: "Excuse my French but fuck 97.9 the Boxx and you know that's our whole thing. ... That's all I'm on [eschewing 97.9 the Boxx] because 97.9 don't represent Houston in any shape form or fashion. You very rarely even hear any artists from Houston being played on the radio station in the city, this city done grown to 6 million people now. You know, out of 6 million people you should have some type of representation" (interview with the author, January 2012).

Yearning to hear local artists, many Houston-based fans turned to internet-based stations, such as Optimo Radio and The Core 94, that played local hip hop around the clock. Houston hip hop has long had a presence on television through Street Flava, a music video show hosted by local disk jockey D-Solo (Darnell Harris). The local scene has a strong web presence through message boards such as TheScrewshop.com and blogs like Dayandadream.

com. Within the last few years, a former middle school classmate of mine, Donnie Houston, has featured local music and preserved history through his YouTube-based Donnie Houston Podcast.

Over the course of thirty years, the Houston hip hop scene has grown to become a culturally vibrant spatial entity. It features a wide variety of participants, places, and institutions rooted in a strong and constantly reinforced cultural identity. The scene's impact has moved beyond the city into the national popular music landscape through the music of rap stars like Toronto's Drake and New York's A$AP Rocky, as well as international pop stars such as Justin Timberlake, who have to some extent embraced the screw sound. Despite its national and global reach, Houston hip hop culture remains firmly tied to the social dynamics of the city's African American working-class space.

One of the core concerns of my study is the function of symbolic constructions of place in hip hop culture. Rather than focusing on the significance of political and economic realities, I examine the symbolic meaning attached to space and place and the role of these meanings in the creation of hip hop culture. Several scholars (Forman 2002, MacDonald 2009) have noted how individuals and groups internalize spatial constructions such as city and neighborhood. I seek to understand how space and place get transformed into cultural product and process.

While hip hop's macro-level national and global impact is an intriguing phenomenon, its micro-level workings lie at the heart of this project. Hip hop continues to function as a localized art form that is practiced by various African American communities around the country. While the pervasiveness of mainstream forms is undeniable, hip hop consumers are interacting with local forms of this tradition as well. Furthermore, localized hip hop forms have unique compositions, meanings, and impacts since they are rooted in the specific social experience of its core consumers. This study also seeks to explore the relationship between African American youth and young adults and the localized hip hop cultures with which they interact.

1

IF YOU GO DOWN TO HOUSTON

You better stay off Lyons Avenue
Because if you go there green
Somewhere down of Jensen
The last time you'll be seen.
—Jukeboy Bonner, "Stay Off Lyons"

I'm grabbing grain, in the turning lane
And I gotta maintain (cause the laws behind me)
I've tried to leave the game, I know I need to change
(I need to re-score again) meet me on Fondren & Main
—Z-Ro, "Fondren and Main"

Jukeboy Bonner was one of Houston's most enigmatic bluesmen. Contrary to popular convention of the time, Bonner was a one-man band, taking the stage armed only with his guitar and harmonica, which he would play simultaneously. Born in small-town Bellville, Texas, Bonner received his nickname "Jukeboy" because he most often performed around Houston in small clubs and after-hours spots known as "juke joints" (Head 2010).

Bonner's music was a perfect fit for the juke-joint crowd. His songs reflected the post-war experience of working-class Black folks in Houston, one rooted in segregation, economic instability, and rising crime. "Stay Off Lyons" is a prime example of his style. The song, first released by Arhoolie Records in 1968, is a cautionary tale of sorts. Bonner warns the imagined listener against traversing Lyons Avenue, the most active street in Houston's notorious Fifth Ward, a neighborhood with a rich history but more popularly known for its high level of poverty and racial segregation as well as for being a hotbed of criminal activity. Bonner suggests a sordid circumstance whereby one could meet a violent end on Lyons. The street was rechristened "Blood

Alley" by locals, and the bodies of the murdered would be discovered on Jensen Drive, yet another infamous Fifth Ward street. With songs like "Stay Off Lyons" as well as the more popular "Struggle Here in Houston," Bonner creatively represented an aspect of the intimate particularities of Black life in Houston, offering his working-class audience songs that interpreted and protested their communal realities.

In a similar vein, though from a different time period and musical genre, is Z-Ro. Born Joseph Wayne McVey, Z-Ro is a bluesy rap artist and singer from Southwest Houston. Z-Ro, a self-described "King of the Ghetto," has become somewhat of a local hero over his twenty-year career. In fact, many of his fans feel that he has an unquestionable commitment to communicating local experience even at the expense of national stardom. Similar to Jukeboy Bonner, Z-Ro's lyrics reflect local, Black working-class experiences, particularly focusing on the complex and sometimes contradictory nature of street life.

In the selection above from the song "Fondren and Main," we find Z-Ro in the midst of an existential crisis of sorts. He is cruising the streets in his car on his way to rescore drugs on the corner of Fondren and Main, two infamous Southwest Houston streets. As he rides, he's engaged in an internal debate regarding his participation in illegal drug dealing. He understands the pitfalls of such activity but nevertheless continues to be drawn to it. Such themes are not uncommon in hip hop, as gangsta rappers have long written raps that problematized drug dealing. But Z-Ro's message is place-specific. By referencing Fondren and Main, he tells a story that can be located. Z-Ro's internal struggle is not an abstraction. His lyrics invoke a particular spatiality, one that grounds his message in the material realities of those within that particular time and place. Like Jukeboy Bonner before him, Z-Ro's music reflects an explicit engagement with African American space in Houston. This is not surprising considering that the local hip hop scene, like the blues scene before it, has been inextricably tied to the civil society enacted in segregated Black settlement spaces throughout the metropolis.

It is impossible to have a true and adequate understanding of Houston hip hop without engaging with the dynamics of the city's African American population. Therefore, in this chapter I offer a spatial overview of African American life in Houston divided in two sections. The first part of the chapter is dedicated to the development of and life within Houston's multifarious

Black settlement spaces. I maintain that Black life in Houston is grounded in a dialectical negotiation of space whereby African Americans are constantly shaping and reshaping their spaces through cultural means. In the second half, after demonstrating the generation of a spatial formation called *the streets* out of Black settlement space, I argue that the ever-present vulnerability within the streets has generated a significant level of territoriality among working class Black males in Houston. This territoriality, as I will show in chapter 2, has had a major impact on the production of hip hop culture within the city.

African American Space in Houston

Houston's African American population is sizable. In fact, at approximately 524,000, Houston has the fifth-largest African American population in the nation. While the size is notable, it must be weighed against the incredibly large population of the city, which currently stands as 2.3 million. According to the United States Census Bureau, African Americans represent 22.8% of the city's population, which makes them Houston's third-largest racial or ethnic community, far behind Hispanic at 44% and non-Hispanic White at 24%, but significantly ahead of the city's fastest growing group, Asian Americans, at 7% (United States Census Bureau 2021).

While African Americans currently reside throughout the city, remnants of segregation remain in the cultural geography of residencies. There are large pockets or zones of African American life situated in three different parts of the city: one to the north, one in the south, and one southwest. These zones are comprised of several interconnected historically and still predominantly Black neighborhoods. Each cluster is situated away from downtown Houston and outside of Loop 610; two dominate spaces of White residential and business life. Colloquially called the Northside, the Southside, and Southwest, these clusters are integral spaces for the production of local African American culture.

Houston's native Black community view the Northside, Southside, and Southwest as legitimate geographical entities. They are the products of Black Houstonians seizing and redefining their segregated sociospatial life through social interaction and discourse. In many ways, they can be seen as similar to political districts—mass constituencies or social bases formed by a curated

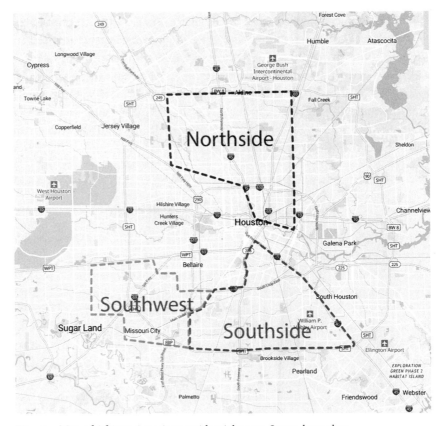

Figure 1. Map of African American residential zones. Image by author.

collection of communities—and have very legitimate implications for residents. Just like political districts, the definition and boundaries of these zones are always in flux and influenced by a variety of factors. For example, in the following quote, Southside resident and Screwed Up Click rapper Lil Randy offers his boundary construction of the Southside: "If you take I-10 and move south, that's the Southside. It don't stop. You can ride all the way to Lake Jackson I ain't gon' lie. I had a closed mind when I was making Screwtapes. To me, back then, I only considered from Gulfgate to 2234, from Gulfgate to Missouri City, that was the Southside. But the Southside is actually bigger than that" (interview with the author, 2012).

Likely due to his changing life circumstances, Lil Randy's conception of the Southside has shifted over the years. This is not at all unique to him. Definitions shift within and between individuals because the boundaries of these Black spaces are not standardized. The Northside, Southside, and Southwest are symbolic spatial sectors that have been actively shaped and defined by Black Houstonians, and these spaces continue to facilitate the sustenance of their collective civic life.

THE NORTHSIDE

The "Northside" of Houston, sometimes referred to as the "Nawf" by residents, is situated immediately north and northeast of Houston's downtown business district. The cluster includes the historic Black neighborhoods of Acres Homes, Kashmere Gardens, Trinity Gardens, Greenspoint, Settegast, the Scenic Woods, and Fifth Ward among others. The center of African American life in the Northside is Fifth Ward, which was among the initial six wards or political divisions established by the city in 1836. First settled by newly freed slaves in the wake of emancipation, African American locals considered Fifth Ward to be the cultural center of Houston's Black American life by the end of World War II. At this time, the neighborhood featured a mix of working-class and middle-class households, which included a large segment of Black creole transplants from Louisiana. As Fifth Ward reached its residential capacity in the 1960s, other Northside neighborhoods including Acres Homes, Kashmere Gardens, and Trinity Gardens were settled and developed along the neighborhood's periphery.

"Northside" neighborhoods are largely working class. The median household income for Fifth Ward is $20,326 (City of Houston 2013b), which is less than half of Houston's average of $42,877 (City of Houston 2013b), and nearly half of the population lives below the poverty level. Contributing to this is unchecked unemployment as nearly 60% of the neighborhood's population is either unemployed or not in the labor force (City of Houston 2013a). Other Northside neighborhoods are faring only slightly better. Acres Homes' median household income is $32,053 (City of Houston 2013b) and nearly half of its population is not working. Settegast's statistics mirror those of Acres Homes. Precarious economic conditions have also led to higher than average crime rates in the Northside. By the mid-1980s, Fifth Ward was nicknamed the "Bloody Nickel" in reference to its high homicide rate and general atmosphere of urban decay (Agee-Aldridge 2014). Greenspoint has been similarly rechristened as "Gunspoint" because of its high rate of violent activity (Martin 2019).

While its economic climate has been dire for over half a century, the Northside has been a vital space for African American creativity in Houston. In particular, Fifth Ward has been the site of a number of Houston's major musical movements. Creole migrants from Louisiana brought zydeco, the accordion-based dance music native to Southwest Louisiana. Early zydeco artists, including L. C. Donnato, Clifton Chenier, and Boozoo Chavis performed in the many small clubs throughout the area—the Continental Zydeco Ballroom most notably. From the 1950s through the 1970s, Fifth Ward had a national recording industry presence through Duke-Peacock Records, which was owned and operated by area native Don Robey and was the recording home of artists such as Big Mama Thornton, Bobby Blue Bland, and Little Richard. Moving away from Fifth Ward, the Kashmere High School's stage band, led by the late Conrad O. Johnson, performed around the country for eighteen years and released a number of notable recordings.

Fifth Ward also proved to be ground zero for the emergence of Houston's local hip hop scene in the mid-1980s. It was the original home of Rap-A-Lot Records, Houston's flagship rap label started by Houston and Fifth Ward native James Smith, aka J. Prince, in 1986. For more than twenty-five years, Rap-A-Lot has released albums by a wealth of local talent including the Geto Boys, Scarface, and Devin the Dude. Swishahouse, the onetime recording home of Northside luminaries Slim Thug, Paul Wall, and Chamillionaire, was also founded in the Northside. The Northside is also home to rappers in the gangsta tradition like the 5th Ward Boyz, Trinity Garden Cartel, and J-Dawg; underground rappers such as D. Risha and Dirty Dog D; and Christian rappers Nuwine and Lil Raskull.

THE SOUTHSIDE

Similarly, the Southside of Houston is a collection of African American neighborhoods situated south of downtown Houston. These neighborhoods include South Park, Sunnyside, South Acres, Cloverland, Hiram Clarke, and its center, Third Ward. Third Ward is the Southside's premier neighborhood. Sociologist Robert D. Bullard, known for his studies of inner city Houston, calls Third Ward "the hub of black social, cultural, and economic life in Houston" (Bullard 1987, 30). Third Ward, or simply "The Trey" as locals call it, boasts approximately 13,000 residents, 70% of whom identify as African American (City of Houston 2012). A number of institutions important to the social life of African Americans in the neighborhood and beyond are within its radius. Texas Southern University, the third largest historically Black college and university in the nation, calls Third Ward its home. In terms of arts and culture, the neighborhood is home to the city's two leading African American visual arts institutions, the Houston Museum of African American Culture and Project Row Houses. Third Ward is also an important center for Black business as a number of Black-owned firms operate out of the neighborhood (Duggins 2000, Boney 2013).

From a socioeconomic standpoint, a duality exists in the Third Ward. An imaginary line divides the neighborhood into two very dissimilar sections. Its southern portion has a solid base of middle- to upper-class residents who occupy homesteads near both Texas Southern University and the University of Houston. These residents include professors, doctors, lawyers, and other professionals who work both within and outside of the neighborhood and are largely responsible for the maintenance of the neighborhood's economic stability. The picture is much different as one moves north. Occupying Texas Southern University's northern border is the Cuney Homes, Houston's oldest low-income public housing unit. If you continue in the same direction, you will encounter several streets of dilapidated apartment complexes and shotgun houses that are inhabited by some of the city's poorest residents. In 2013, a section along the neighborhood's northern perimeter, at the intersection of McGowan and Dowling streets, was named the fifteenth most dangerous neighborhood in America (Stanton 2013).

Third Ward was among the earliest political districts established after Houston's independence in 1836. By 1930, the populations of African Americans and Whites in Third Ward were nearly equal. At this time, the African American portion of the neighborhood featured a solid mix of middle-class and working-class households. After World War II, the majority of the area's White residents moved into new housing developments in the suburbs, which resulted in the Third Ward becoming a majority Black space. By the 1960s,

Third Ward had become a vital space for Black enterprise and entertainment. Storied businesses such as Frenchy's Restaurant, Wolf's Department Store, and Riverside Bank opened their doors during this period. Many of these residents chose to spend their money at the area's numerous entertainment venues—such as Shady's Playhouse and the Eldorado Ballroom—where they enjoyed the musical styles of artists like local blues legends Albert Collins and Sam "Lightenin'" Hopkins, who immortalized the neighborhood in his 1965 song "I Was Down on Dowling Street" (Wood 2003).

As Third Ward reached its residential capacity in the 1960s, African Americans began occupying spaces that surrounded the neighborhood. Some Blacks moved into less dense neighborhoods such as Sunnyside, which was an unincorporated African American community before being annexed by the city. Others moved into formerly predominantly White neighborhoods such as Hiram Clarke, converting them over time to spaces of Black life.

Like Hiram Clarke, the Southside neighborhood of South Park was originally developed as a White American enclave. As journalist Katharine Shilcutt notes, "the neighborhood was created in the 1950s for middle-class whites and their baby boomer kids. A reflection of the postwar time period and of the homebuyers themselves—who were mostly returning war veterans" (2011). The late 1960s, spurred on by the construction of Loop 610 and forced integration, saw an influx of African American residents and outflux of Whites who moved to suburban Pearland and Pasadena. By the early 1980s, South Park had become one of the largest Black communities in Houston. Currently, the neighborhood is home to 21,280 residents, 71% of whom are Black (City of Houston 2012).

Over the last twenty years, some residents of the South Park neighborhood have been engaged in a discursive quarrel with Fifth Ward residents for the title of "toughest neighborhood in the city." Longstanding economic instability has fueled its desolate atmosphere. The neighborhood's economy quickly eroded as the result of economic oppression as well as a series of flights: first the neighborhood's original White residents, followed by its Black middle class, who moved to suburban areas in the 1980s. Subsequently, underground economics soared as South Park became ground zero for the crack cocaine trade. Shilcutt suggests that South Park almost "cannibalized" itself via its unchecked violent crime (2011). As rapper Cl'Che of the South Park Coalition told journalist Lance Scott Walker, after the middle-class flight South Park "started having more drug affiliations, more robberies, burglaries, killings, and more children doing things they gotta do as far as prostitution and so forth" (Walker 2013, 461). During my time in the field, South Park's median household income was $28,951, among the lowest in the city (City of Houston 2013b). This was driven by rampant unemployment as 55% of adults 16 and over were without work (City of Houston 2013a).

Poverty and crime are most certainly problems, yet, at the same time, South Park has long been a prime space for Black working-class expression. The neighborhood is home to a multitude of institutions that have become synonymous with Black working-class life in Houston. MacGregor Park has long been a primary public spot of socialization for youth in South Park even though it is technically situated outside the borders of the neighborhood. Across its 82 acres are running trails, basketball courts, tennis courts, and a baseball diamond, all of which are busy from morning into night. King's Flea Market is less than a mile away from MacGregor Park and has been a primary retail space within the Southside for many decades. At King's, one could purchase everything from the latest fashions to car rims from local and primarily Black retailers. In addition, South Park features several small clubs and after-hours spots that serve its adult population.

South Park and other Southside neighborhoods have been vital to the emergence and growth of hip hop culture in Houston. These neighborhoods have produced many Houston hip hop luminaries including DJ Screw (South Park), K-Rino (South Park), Fat Pat (South Park), Devin the Dude (Third Ward), Scarface (South Acres), Lil Flip (Cloverland) and Big Mello (Hiram Clarke) among many others. The Southside also features many of the scene's most treasured institutions. Nestled in Hiram Clarke is Screwed Up Records & Tapes, the record store once owned and operated by the late DJ Screw,[1] the chief cultivator of Houston hip hop's local identity by way of the screwed and chopped music scene and one of its most respected figures both within and outside of Houston. The store has long been an important social space for Houston rap artists and has become a tourist attraction for non-Houstonians interested in the culture. Big Tyme Records, an independent hip hop record store housed inside of King's Flea Market, is also notable. While an important retail entity, Big Tyme once operated as a recording label, releasing albums by Houston-based rap artists DJ Screw, Underground Kingz (UGK), and Psk-13 among others. These stores, along with the many studios and performance venues scattered throughout the area, make the Southside a key center for hip hop production in Houston.

SOUTHWEST

A new zone of Black life has emerged in Southwest Houston over the last thirty years. African Americans make up a significant portion of Southwest Houston's neighborhoods such as Westbury, Alief, and Sharpstown, as well as spaces in Missouri City, a suburb of Houston. This new zone is the result of increasing suburbanization of the city's Black population beginning in the 1980s as middle-class Blacks followed by working-class Blacks began populating neighborhoods in the Southwest that were at one time predominantly White. While there are some new majority Black neighborhoods in the area, most African Americans live amongst White and Hispanic Houstonians as well as the area's ever-expanding immigrant population, and most often in the many low-income apartment complexes scattered through the area.

The Southwest lacks the history and cultural institutions that define Black life in the Northside and Southside. Schools, especially those within the Alief and Houston Independent school districts, are primary spaces of community building for Black Americans in the Southwest. Prior to its closure and conversion into PlazAmericas flea market, Sharpstown Mall, a large-scale shopping center in the Sharpstown neighborhood, was another important social space for Black residents. In recent years, the area has become a bastion of Black nightclubs, after-hours clubs, and strip clubs.

The Southwest has also been a hot spot for local hip hop culture. Rappers Lil O, Z-Ro, and Trae tha Truth of the Screwed Up Click hail from the area. Lately, it has been a breeding ground for local artists who have made national impacts. It is also home to international hip hop superstar and pop culture icon Travis Scott, who signed to Kanye West's Good Music record label in 2012. His most recent album, *Astroworld*, debuted at #1 on the *Billboard* 200 pop chart in 2018. It is also home to Maxo Kream and Tobe Nwigwe, two children of Nigerian immigrants who have garnered much buzz over the last few years.

Black Settlement Space

While informal in nature, the Northside, Southside, and Southwest are what Stephen Nathan Haymes calls "black settlement spaces." According to Haymes, Black settlement space is "the location from which urban blacks

construct alternative experiences of time, space, and interpersonal relationships or community" (Haymes 1995, 13). Houston's Black settlement spaces
are self-contained geographic divisions that feature a multitude of social
service buildings, commercial districts, and spaces for social and musical
interaction that serve several interconnected neighborhoods. Residents from
all over the Southside, for example, patronize Third Ward's central business
district, which includes the legendary clothier Wolf's Department Store as
well as the iconic Frenchy's Restaurant. In the 1980s and '90s, Martin Luther
King Boulevard in South Park was vital entertainment space for the Southside with numerous nightclubs and record stores that featured southern soul
and early hip hop. Multiservice centers, buildings that contain a variety of
civil resources, are in nearly every Southside neighborhood. The same is
true of the Northside, which features Homestead and Lockwood streets as
important social areas.

   "Houston is a big place, geographically," Justice Allah once told me. "So
just being that spread out, it kind of limited people from being able to travel
because most of these neighborhoods was poor, impoverished neighborhoods" (interview with the author, January 2012). As Allah suggests, Houston
is a geographically sizable city, which, combined with its intricate highway
system, makes traveling a difficult task for all citizens, especially members
of the working class. For example, Northside's Fifth Ward is 17 miles away
from Southside's South Park. In order to travel between the two neighborhoods, one has to use a series of congested freeways. This trip is, at minimum,
twenty-five minutes via private car during a low-traffic period. For members
of the working class, the lack of private vehicles and Houston's substandard
public transit system add to the difficulty of such cross-town trips. Screwed
Up Click member Lil Randy, who grew up in South Park, describes traveling to the Northside as a "big adventure" that would happen no more than
once a month (interview with the author, April 2012). As a result, Black
Houstonians have historically socialized primarily within their immediate
settlement spaces.

   Restricted mobility, both social and physical, has contributed to high levels
of place attachment among African American Houstonians. M. Carmen Hidalgo and Bernardo Hernandez define place attachment as "the effective bond
or link between people and specific places" (Hidalgo and Hernandez 2001,
274). Place attachments denote the emotional connection between individuals

and their physical environments. These bonds can be generated through a variety of mechanisms that include habitual engagements with environments and neighbors, physically personalizing a space, celebrations that occur in a space, and more (Brown, Perkins, and Brown 2003, 259). Regarding Houston's African American community, sociologist Henry Bullock notes, "People of one area associate more with each other than with people of other areas. Their loyalty toward each other is stronger, and they are definitely oriented toward their areas in terms of more immediate needs" (Bullock 1957, 64). These bonds are primarily developed during adolescence, when socialization is at its peak and mobility is restricted. Such socialization occurs in youth-oriented public spaces such as parks, recreation centers, skating rinks, and teen clubs. High schools have, historically, been one of the foremost vehicles for the development of these social networks as they are spaces that facilitate the consistent comingling of kids from different neighborhoods. Jack Yates High School, for instance, serves students from Third Ward, Yellowstone, and a portion of South Park. Kashmere High School includes students from Kashmere Gardens and Trinity Gardens. These school-facilitated bonds are most pronounced within the field of high school athletics. While there are rivalries between schools within the same geographical zone, games between Northside and Southside schools are the most intense. Bullard states: "Strong competition and rivalries probably are most pronounced in athletic competitions, developed among the various black neighborhoods. The athletic rivalry between Phyllis Wheatley High School, in Fifth Ward, and Jack Yates High School, in Third Ward, epitomized this competition. The competition between those two schools represented more than a sports event or game and held the emotions of the entire Houston black community" (1987, 27).

The intense atmosphere surrounding such athletic competitions reflects the investment Black Houstonians have in their respective neighborhoods. Competitions bring the spatially dislocated networks together, making social divisions explicit and, for the victorious side, allowing cultural dominance to be asserted, even if it is only temporary. In Houston, neighborhoods are much more than residential and activity spaces; they represent social networks that bond residents to one another based on shared space and experience.

Central to understanding Houston's Black settlement space is Henri Lefebvre's (1991) concept of "social space." As discussed in the introduction, social space is a complex and socially constructed product that involves three separate but interacting spatial entities: representations of space (conceived space), representational spaces (lived space), and spatial practices (perceived space). "Conceived space" is the realm of government officials, city planners, architects, and others with culturally defined power to impose order and control within a space. "Lived space" functions in the experiential realm and relates to the symbolic meanings attached to space by its inhabitants. "Perceived space" (or spatial practice) can also be considered "place" (Agnew 2011, 324) and includes material or physical sites within spaces such as streets, corners, stores, houses, neighborhoods, and cities. It also refers to the sites and social activities that make up our daily routines or everyday life. Place (or perceived space) can be entered, traversed, and mapped. "Perceived space" is where ideas and experiences of space become concrete.

Lefebvre spends much of his book *The Production of Space* discussing the ways in which capitalist societies, through governmental practices, have dominated spatial production and "colonized" everyday life through spatial practices and representations of space (Agnew 2011, 18). Houston's segregated civic space is a good example of this. De jure and then de facto segregation determined where African Americans were allowed to be situated in the city. White urban planners created each and every one of these historic Black neighborhoods. The segregation was reinforced by a transit system that literally isolated the African American community from the rest of the city.

Lefebvre argues from an explicitly Marxist standpoint that subjugated people will actively push back against such spatial domination in the lived realm. This process is articulated further by Diane Chisholm, who argues that "the making of livable space entails the constant struggle by city dwellers to appropriate and re-appropriate space for purposes other than means-end productivity and official traffic and trade" (Chisholm 2005, 28). Black Houstonians, with their creation of the Southside, Northside, and Southwest, have taken spaces of domination and symbolically turned them into sites of social autonomy, affirmation, and empowerment. Even though the physical structures and social interactions remain overwhelmingly informed by governmental economic and bureaucratic practices, Black Houstonians actively seek to control the meaning of their spaces. They have created what Lefebvre calls a "differential space" or what can be considered an oppositional space that rejects material realities in favor of symbolic value. They have even named their differential spaces—Northside, Southside, and Southwest—to reflect their ownership of them. Such measures are not unique to Houston. According to Stephen Nathan Haymes, Black Americans "define and use urban space to renegotiate an oppositional identity which knits together neighbors and draws families together across the city" (Haymes 1995, 112). While never escaping domination, Black Houstonians have created a counter-discourse that challenges their material subjugation by allowing them to feel and exert some sense of control over their space.

2

EVERYBODY INHERITS THE HOOD

OG Scott might as well be the mayor of Cloverland, a small predominantly African American neighborhood in Southeast Houston. He is the essence of servitude. When I first met him, he invited me to come to an Easter Egg hunt that he organizes yearly for the neighborhood youth. This is on top of the countless social and service events that he regularly throws, on his own, funded primarily with his own money. Along with food, toys, and school supplies, Scott also provides advice and guidance to neighborhood youth and adults. His house on Botany Lane is a neighborhood hub. Community people flock there for advice, entertainment, and fellowship. OG Scott is what all young people should aspire to be in an ideal world. He is a pillar of his community in the truest sense. He holds everyone up and holds the community down.

OG is not a nickname, however. It's a title. To be an O.G. signifies that the holder has knowledge, wisdom, and especially experience. The O.G. has been tested in battle and has continued to survive. This is certainly true for OG Scott. Flash back thirty years and you will find a teenage Scott living on Botany Lane and in the same house. The garage is still his hangout spot and neighbors are still moving in and out of it at all times of day. But instead of advice or a helping hand, this younger Scott is dispensing a new drug called crack cocaine. "I was making $2500 a day, standing here in this basement. I'm talkin' 'rock for rock,'" he tells me. Scott's entrance into the drug game was rather unremarkable. Hungry one night, he reached out to his older brother for money for food. Instead of dollars, however, Scott's brother offered him a nugget of crack to sell. He was initially hesitant, but the challenge, his curiosity, and hunger eventually won out. He carefully cut the nugget up into little servings and sold them to the parade of neighborhood addicts who moved up and down the streets. Upon selling out, Scott realized that he had hit a financial windfall. "By the time my brother had gotten home, I had made about six or seven hundred dollars off of about seventy dollars worth of shit. That's the way it was from then on" (OG Scott, interview with the author, 2012).

Scott was among the many Cloverland residents who got swept up in the various sides of the crack game. "Crack changed the whole Cloverland. Guys that were chemists. Guys that went to Harvard. That shit brought them down," he says. "But it brought the youngsters up." These youngsters were making significant amounts of money selling crack in Cloverland and they did not hesitate to spoil themselves from the riches of their trade. Scott and friends outfitted themselves in designer clothes and decadent jewelry. When they were not being transported by limousine services, they challenged each other in race cars and in the construction of customized cars. This culture of decadence was met with an equally pervasive culture of violence, however. The drug game generated violent robberies, car jackings, and gun battles over territory.

Scott and other Botany Lane drug dealers eventually moved away from the drug game to more legitimate and safer occupations. Their experiences and exploits, however, were immortalized in the hip hop music that emerged from the neighborhood. Hip hop and crack emerged in Cloverland at approximately the same time. Neighborhood rap artists joined dealers in neighborhood social spaces and naturally began documenting neighborhood street life in their reality-based rhymes. For instance, according to OG Scott, legendary local rap group the Botany Boyz were a group of neighborhood kids who hung out in drug territory and eventually would rap about the lives of Scott and others in their rhymes. Similar things happened in Third Ward, Sunnyside, South Park, and other Southside neighborhoods. As a result, Houston street life and Houston hip hop culture became inextricably bound in a reciprocal fashion. Houston hip hop heritage has a very distinct character that is rooted in Houston street practices, namely slab culture, lean use, and screwed & chopped music. More explicitly, Houston street life gave Houston hip hop its unique local sound and character.

THEORIZING "THE STREET"

In Houston, and other urban locales around the country, economic instability has influenced the development of two culturally significant spaces:
the 'hood and the street. The "'hood" is a term that emerged among post-
industrial, working-class Black youth to affirmatively define their areas of
experience. The 'hood can be of any scale, from apartment building to streets,
blocks, whole neighborhoods, or groups of neighborhoods. One's 'hood includes the people, homes, churches, parks, businesses, and other elements
important to a person. Short for neighborhood, *'hood* marks the places that
were traditionally labeled as "ghetto," a term propagated within mainstream
spaces to demarcate the most undesirable and detested racialized spaces in
an urban environment. Within this context, the ghetto is defined by poverty, violence, and assorted deviance, all of which are considered products
of a community's failure to meet socioeconomic standards. The ghetto is to
be feared, surveilled, ridiculed, and quarantined. In this way, the term is a
form of discursive dominance. With *'hood*, post–Civil Rights Black youth
have pushed back against the reductive and pejorative "ghetto" label and
promoted a spatial identity that better reflects their deep attachment to and
identification with their areas of experience (Forman 2002, 65).

"The streets" are spaces grafted onto 'hoods in Houston and inner cities
around the United States actively generated by young African American men
and women whose social practices stand in opposition to mainstream society's. The streets can be considered as a subordinate space of the 'hood and
are composed of street corners, nightclubs, parks, private homes, storefronts,
or anywhere this particular alienated segment of men and women congregate
for economic and recreational activity. It is marked by the particular social
identities, attitudes, and practices that occur within its fluid bounds. Within
"the streets," narcotics distribution is a key economic channel. Interpersonal
violence works to reinforce both the economic system and an individual's
social standing within the community. Unique "street" language, dress, and
recreational practices also exist. As their social activity alienates them from
larger society, this particular segment of Black youth, men, and women use
public and private settings within their 'hoods to enact their collective social
life, thus creating a space called the streets.

Many scholars have tackled the concept of *the streets*, but these studies
by and large focus solely on subcultural attributes. The spatial nature of the

concept is often underexplored or not mentioned at all. William Oliver, in his article "The Streets: An Alternative Black Male Socialization Institution," is one of the few who highlights the importance of space and place in explicating the concept. Though never explicitly labeling it a space, Oliver's description of the streets highlights their spatiality: "'the streets' is used here to refer to the network of public and semipublic social settings (e.g., street corners, vacant lots, bars, clubs, after-hours joints, convenience stores, drug houses, pool rooms, parks and public recreational places, etc.) in which primarily lower and working-class Black males tend to congregate" (2006, 919). Oliver adds that within this network of settings, young Black men are inculcated with an oppositional set of attitudes and practices that, for him, include underemployment, poverty, substance abuse, and incarceration. For Oliver, the street is a type of socialization institution that competes with other such institutions, including family, school, and church, for psychological prominence among Black men in the inner city. In a similar vein, sociologist Elijah Anderson (1999) intimates the spatiality of *streets* through his concept of "staging areas," hangout spots where young people come together to engage in the attitudes, practices, and identities associated with *the street*.

The streets is a socially constructed space. *The streets* involves an appropriation of places within Black neighborhoods and is therefore constantly in flux in terms of constitution and engagement. The settings that make up the streets—street corners, nightclubs, parks, and more—are only considered part of the streets if there is street activity occurring within them. For instance, by day, a park can function as a site for the traditional socialization of children. By night, however, drug activity occurring within the park grounds turns the park into a component of the streets. When in the streets, individuals must adhere to the accepted standards of the space. However, when they are outside the streets, they are less beholden to street expectations.

Insiders and outsiders of the streets are very conscious of what is meant by "the streets" as well as its meaning for their lives. For example, when I asked local rap artist Big Al to detail his life growing up in the Northside's Lakewood neighborhood, he succinctly replied, "I was in the streets" (interview with the author, 2012). Legendary Houston rapper and producer Icey Hott notes that the members of his group Street Military came "out of the streets" (interview with the author, 2011). In these statements, both Big Al and Icey

Hott intend to make reference to their engagement with street-related activities. However, their use of the signifiers "in" and "out" highlights that these activities are contained within geographic and social space. In short, street occupants understand *the streets* as a space of sociological and psychological relevance.

HOUSTON STREET CULTURE

The streets, in general, are the products of social and economic ruptures at the federal, state, and local levels. For example, in New York, the South Bronx streets of the 1960s and 1970s, which fueled the rise of hip hop culture, were produced by municipal urban renewal programs that sought to transform Manhattan into a competitive enterprise zone. This parallels the production of the Blood and Crip gang-identified streets of Los Angeles, which were spurred by a transformation of inner-city economies and the movement of factories from the inner city to suburban and foreign land, a problem exacerbated by the dismantling of important social welfare programs during the Reagan administration.

The Houston streets of the 1980s and early 1990s was the result of a convergence of social phenomena beginning with a large-scale out-migration of middle-class Blacks from predominantly African American neighborhoods in the early 1970s. Spurred by the passage of the city's Fair Housing Ordinance, which outlawed discrimination in the sale, rental, and financing of houses, upwardly mobile Blacks began to move from these predominantly Black spaces into White and mixed-race neighborhoods (Bullard 1987, 54). In *When Work Disappears* (1997) sociologist William Julius Wilson notes that such middle-class flight disrupts the economies and social organization of predominantly Black neighborhoods. For Houston's Black neighborhoods, this meant population decrease and small-business erosion. Howard Beeth and Cary Wintz note that because of middle-class flight, the "self-contained black communities—with their small-town atmosphere that was common in the early twentieth century—ceased to exist" (1992, 165).

Exacerbating matters was an oil market–based recession that swept through Houston in the early 1980s. Since the discovery of oil near Houston in 1901, the local economy had been increasingly dependent on oil production. By the early 1970s, oil production had become the center of the local economy, and high world oil prices made Houston a boomtown, a space of significant economic and population growth. However, an increase in global oil production combined with a domestic decrease in demand caused oil prices to drop sharply in the early 1980s (Eaton 2016, Wray 2020). Houston, once a hub for United States oil production, felt the downturn more than other cities. Failure in the oil sector negatively impacted other segments of the local economy, leading to a full-out recession by the mid-1980s. Journalist Aaron Latham writes, "when the price of oil went up in the seventies, it made Houston rich. When the price went down in the eighties, it made Houston poor—at least poorer. A lot of the bang went out of the boom town" (1985). Houston's Black community was severely affected by this economic downturn. According to Robert Bullard, "the economic recession of the 1980s contributed to a double-digit unemployment rate in black Houston" (1987). By 1986, the Black unemployment rate stood at 12.5 percent, compared to 5.7 percent for Whites. During the same period, more than 20 percent of Houston's Black population lived below the poverty line.

Middle-class flight and local recession undermined African American communities in Houston. Formerly comprising a mix of classes, these neighborhoods now consisted of an isolated working class and the poor. Local and federal efforts to cut the spread of poverty, such as the Community Development Block Grant program and the Houston Job Training and Partnership Council, were mostly ineffective. Neighborhoods such as South Park, Sunny Side, Acres Home, and Fifth Ward, once vital areas of Black life, were now full of hopelessness and despair.

The situation was made worse when crack emerged in the mid-1980s. Crack became the dominant drug in inner cities across America shortly after its emergence. The reasons behind this are twofold, according to sociologists Craig Reinarman and Harry G. Levine. First, crack was powerful, yet cheap to produce, which matched well with the finances of the impoverished and their desire for immediate escape. The second reason relates to the economic situation of the inner city: "there was a huge workforce of unemployed young people ready to take jobs in the new, neighborhood-based business of crack preparation and sales. Working in the crack business offered these people better jobs, working conditions, and pay than any 'straight' job they could get" (Reinarman and Levine 1997, 2). Unable to attain legitimate employment, many young Black men saw the crack trade as a viable job option.

While an arresting force for many in the community, crack cocaine proved to be an economic boon for many formerly economically marginalized young Black men in Houston. At the very least, these dealers were able to achieve a base level of economic stability for themselves and their families. At the most, they attained relative wealth. As a result, these drug dealers, or D-boys as they became known, had significant social influence among youth and young adults. "Every neighborhood had what we would call, 'a D-boy,'" says Houston-based rapper E.S.G. "And a D-boy, pretty much, influences his whole neighborhood" (interview with the author, 2012). In Cloverland, young men would gather up and down its two-block span to fellowship and learn the ways of the street. Scott pointed out to me that members of the legendary Houston rap group the Botany Boyz were among these youths. Despite the fact that they named themselves after Botany Lane, none of them had lived on the street, according to Scott. They were simply among the other "buck wild-ass kids" who hung on the corner of Botany Lane and Letrim Way in close proximity to the D-boys they idolized (OG Scott, interview with the author, April 2012).

Recreation and fellowship were important aspects of Southside street life. Dealers and other types of street hustlers understood the importance of work-life balance. They congregated in various social spaces throughout the Southside. "We would see each other in the streets," P Izm the Mack told me. "We would congregate at different places until the cops ran us off" (interview with the author, 2013). There were Southside-based nightclubs and strip clubs such as Club 808, Sokol Village, King Leos, and Carrington's, also known as Carros. After-hours clubs were also popular. These were clubs that were legally allowed to stay open after the city's 2 am entertainment curfew—with one caveat: they were not allowed to sell alcohol. The street community frequented after-hours clubs because it allowed them to party while others slept. They were relatively safe and discrete social institutions.

King's Flea Market was another popular hangout spot. Occupying the corner of Griggs and Calhoun until 2014, King's was a flea market in the most traditional sense. It was a large, open building where small business owners could rent out space to sell their wares. In the 1970s, immigrant vendors used King's to sell vegetables, fruit, and other products for domestic use. By the mid-1980s, however, these same immigrant vendors were capitalizing on the flashiness of crack-dealing culture by selling gold jewelry, fine urban fashions, and even expensive vehicle rims. King's Flea Market became popular among dealers, pimps, and other hustlers eager to display the spoils of their trades.

MacGregor Park could be considered the most iconic social space within the Houston streets. The spacious park occupies 83 acres of land bordered by Calhoun Road, Old Spanish Trail, and Martin Luther King Jr Blvd near South Park. It has all the amenities common to neighborhood parks. It has an incredible amount of green space that neighborhood folk use to host cookouts throughout the year. Area residents use the park's public pool to cool off from the sweltering heat that punishes Houston year-round. NBA and street ball legends have honed their skills on the basketball courts that sit next to the park's recreation center. The park is also home to the Homer Ford Tennis Center, which houses the legendary MacGregor Park tennis program. It also includes Neagle Field, the office field for the Texas Southern Universities baseball team. I can personally attest to MacGregor Park's importance to African American social life in the area. My grandmother's house is right around the corner from MacGregor Park. During my frequent visits to her house, I would go to the park to ride bikes and play catch among other things.

MacGregor Park was, and continues to be, an important space for Black civil society in Houston. However, in the 1980s and 90s, it was also central to a generation of local Black street culture. "Everybody went to MacGregor Park," P Izm says. "Guys would just roll and post up, and girls would come through lookin' sexy" (interview with the author, 2013). The most successful drug dealers gathered at the park on Sundays to show off their modified cars, jeeps, and bikes. While there, these dealers and others from the 'hood enjoyed the R&B, funk, and hip hop sounds spun by local DJ Darryl Scott. Martin Luther King Boulevard (formerly South Park Boulevard) also became the site for these impromptu and informal parties.

The crack markets of the 1980s fueled the development of *the streets* within the Southside of Houston as drug dealers, pimps, and others drawn to the social world from 'hoods such as Cloverland, South Park, and Hiram Clarke created spaces for their economic and social activities. The same phenomenon occurred on the Northside within 'hoods like Fifth Ward, Trinity Gardens, and Acres Homes. Though an insular social formation, the streets radically altered life in the 'hood and birthed indigenous practices that would come to influence both Black civil society and later local hip hop culture.

One such practice is sippin syrup. Also called "lean" and "drank," syrup is the prescription-strength codeine-based cough syrup concoction that became popular on the streets of Houston in the late 1980s. Users often combine 2 ounces (called a deuce) or 4 ounces (called a fo') of syrup with either a soft drink, liquor, or candy and drink the thick and muddy concoction out of double Styrofoam cups, a single cup being too weak to contain the heavy liquid. The effect of the drug is a woozy state, where all senses are greatly slowed. Users experience a heightened sense of euphoria and a loss of equilibrium that causes them to lean over, which is why this altered state produced by the drug is known as "leanin." The recreational use of cough syrup predates contemporary Houston street culture. As local rapper-singer Adrian E. told me, "It's been around a long time. When I started bringing it around [in the 1990s], I can remember my parents squaring me off like, 'nigga, we know what you're doin. I drank cough syrup before.' It always been around" (interview with the author, 2012). The drug rose to prominence in the early 1990s among drug dealers who could afford to buy the relatively expensive drug through bogus prescriptions or off the black market. Syrup would eventually become a core part of local hip hop identity and one of the dominant images of the Houston hip hop scene at the national level.

Slab, a modified car practice, is another core practice within Houston street culture. Slab cars commonly are large-bodied American sedans that feature multi-layered paint jobs, dynamic exterior alterations, three-dimensional trunk displays, and explosive sound systems. The name "slab" is related to the sheer amount of external additions, which weigh the cars down to the concrete slabs of the street. Slab owners invest thousands of dollars in the creation of their vehicles, purchasing their cars when they are in modest states and slowly converting them into something more elaborate. During this process, the vehicle becomes inscribed with individual experience and identity and broadcasts this to the outside world. At the center of its rise was the emergence of the 84-type "swangas," the thirty-spoke chrome rims that came standard on the 1984 Cadillac Eldorado. Deemed a road hazard, they were only produced for a single year, making them extremely rare and highly valuable. Swangas were very popular within the streets because of their exclusivity. In the late 1980s and early 1990s, the wheels and slabs were status symbols for Southside street guys like Toast, Corey Blount, and the Bubba Twins. These cars allowed them to increase their social influence within the neighborhood.

SUBCULTURAL CAPITAL IN THE HOUSTON STREETS

The space of the streets is not the site of structureless social activity. As in any social formation, practices within the streets are informed by a larger set of social processes. Sociologist Sarah Thornton's concept of subcultural capital, which she introduces in her seminal work *Club Cultures: Music, Media, and Subcultural Capital* (1996), is a useful framework for analyzing the social processes taking place in the streets. *Subcultural capital* refers to the collective objects, practices, and knowledge that can "confer status on its owner in the eyes of a relevant beholder" (Thornton 1996, 11). It is a type of social currency that determines where one fits in the social hierarchy of one's particular social formations. It determines who is considered an insider and who is considered an outsider, or who is popular or unpopular. Within the streets, it can regulate the respected versus the vulnerable.

In the streets, subcultural capital is accumulated and exchanged for respect, the ultimate form of power. In *Code of the Street: Decency, Violence, and the Moral Life of the Inner City*, Elijah Anderson defines respect as "being granted the proper due or deference one deserves" (1999, 33). Respect is a core catalyst in building and maintaining self-esteem for those in the streets. It can protect one, to a certain extent, from violent encounters. It is for these reasons that "respect is fought for and held and challenged as much as honor was in the age of chivalry" (Anderson 1999, 66). Daunte, a former member of Houston rap group the Bloc Boyz Click, echoes this notion in colloquial fashion, explaining that "everyone wants to be 'the nigga' in their 'hood" (interview with the author, 2012). Being "the nigga" means one who is among the most respected persons in his or her area and therefore wields a certain amount of power.

Violence is one of the primary ways young men can gain respect in the streets. In such spaces, street actors seek to build and develop violent reputations for themselves, as both a preventative and mobility measure. For street actors, "their very identity, their self-respect, and their honor are often intricately tied up with the way they perform on the streets during and after such violent encounters. And it is this identity, including a credible reputation for payback, or vengeance, that is strongly believed to deter future assaults" (Anderson 1999, 76). Any challenge or physical assault must be met with violence. Among the middle and upper classes, walking away from a fight is often acceptable and even considered proper protocol. In the streets, it is a crucial violation of cultural standards that could leave one vulnerable. Violent offenses, such as armed robberies and stickups, bring both economic capital and high levels of respect. In addition, simply having a tough or violent demeanor can be beneficial. Perception is what is ultimately important. Street actors want others to believe that they have an aptness for violence. Whether it is by proving oneself victor in a violent encounter or taking someone else's possessions, the most respected individuals within the street are those from whom the threat of violence is the highest.

In a moderately less threatening fashion, material possessions can work to procure respect. Items such as fine clothing, jewelry, and cars can improve status in two ways. First, similar to mainstream culture, they are explicit markers of culturally defined economic success. Possession of these objects reflects an ability to build a significant amount of personal wealth in a space where money is fleeting. Second, and more importantly, they substantiate one's perceived toughness. These items often draw the attention of active carjack artists, stickup men, or others seeking an economic windfall. Therefore, one cannot own and display these material objects without being able to "hold them down," or defend them. In the streets of Houston, slab car culture functions this way. Costing between $10,000 and $50,000 to construct, the vehicles are explicit markers of wealth; however, their components, especially their wheels, are readily resold for high amounts in the underground market, and that makes them popular targets for carjackers. Riding slab is a risk, and those who can safely do so receive much respect within the streets.

The struggle for respect has led to high levels of territoriality within the streets. Territoriality, as defined by geographer Robert Sack, is "the attempt by an individual or group (x) to influence, affect, or control objects, people, and relationships (y) by delimiting and asserting control over a geographic area" (1983, 55). It is a process by which societal impetuses cause individuals or groups to defend and control their social space. In working-class and poor formations, territoriality results from a lack of accessible other forms of capital. As former dealer-turned-gangsta-rapper-turned-Christian-rapper Lil Raskull plainly stated to me, "You know in the 'hood, man, we don't have anything. So everybody inherits the 'hood. And you protect it like it's your own" (interview with the author, July 2012). There are no prerequisites to owning the 'hood. In this world, your neighborhood, street, or whatever you call home becomes your birthright. While not "owning" the 'hood through official means, such as home or business ownership, people do own the social relationships that occur within the neighborhood, as well as the meanings they get from them. Like any valuable possession, the 'hood is both claimed and championed as well as defended from those who literally or figuratively seek to do it harm.

In the Houston streets, the psychological state of territoriality takes active form in the practice of "repping the 'hood." Arguably one of the street's most pervasive practices, "repping the 'hood" involves exhibiting explicit attachment and identification with your neighborhood or primary social area. This "reppin" sometimes happens verbally, especially during instances of interpersonal confrontations as individuals vociferously reference their neighborhoods as verbal support for their physical prowess. At other times, it happens nonverbally. Individuals wear apparel such as T-shirts, jerseys, jackets, and hats bearing their neighborhood's real name or some culturally derived nickname. It is also common for people to display neighborhood hand signs and even tattoo the neighborhood name on their torso. Such reppin' can typically be seen in public areas. As Elijah Anderson notes, "people from other neighborhoods who come to a staging area and present themselves are said to be 'representing' both who they are and the 'world' or 'hood' from which they hail" (1999, 77).

Reppin' the 'hood is an embodiment of space. As one reps their 'hood, they seek to draw upon the perceived characteristics of their 'hood. The reputation of the neighborhood acts as an additive to their individual street reputations. As Elijah Anderson further notes, "people are likely to assume that a person who comes from a 'bad' area is bad" (1999, 77). Rapper Justice Allah has lived in several predominantly Black neighborhoods and knows the social dynamics of the community very well. He articulated the reputation process metaphorically in the following way: "Well, you know, people associate it with you like your success rate, like a team. You know? If you in New York, you say you a Yankee, people associate you with being a winner. They can love you or hate you, which people do, but they know that 'hey man, these guys done won a lot of [World] Series.' So I think your city and your side of town is kind of associated with you, it adds on to your strength. You know" (Justice Allah, interview with the author, 2012). Justice Allah's use of the sports team metaphor is meaningful considering the competitive nature of inner-city life. A sports team collectively competes to achieve certain goals—winning games and eventually a championship of some sort. While not as intentional or cooperative as a sports team, the 'hood works in a similar way. The collective street activity within a neighborhood comes to define it. The amount of violence, drug dealing, and illicit wealth within a neighborhood determines its "success rate" or its social relevance within the larger spatial formation that it is situated in. This "success rate" becomes one of the determining factors in the amount of respect one possesses.

In the Houston streets, protecting territory functions as a collective way to earn respect. There is strength in numbers and by collectively working to claim, defend, and promote the 'hood, each resident can boost their own amount of respect in the streets. Such territorial measures are commonly done through force. Members of the Houston rap group the Bloc Boyz Click, who record for OG Scott's Cloverland Records, told me that they all had to deal with territorial conflicts during their youth. For example, rapper/singer Adrian E. was raised in TABB City, a colloquialism for the four streets that form a square near Hobby Airport in Southeast Houston: Telephone Road, Airport Boulevard, Belfort, and Broadway. While there are a few single-family residences, the area is dominated by several large low-income apartment complexes that house mostly Black residents. Adrian recalls constant involvement in territorial grudges as a youth:

> I remember when I was about nine, ten, or eleven the apartment complexes used to beef with each other. You know, just stupid shit. And I can remember one of my partner's jaw getting broke in a fight we had [with another apartment complex]. And I'm silly because I don't even live in these apartment complexes. I live in a house down the street. So I'm riding my bike down the street to this nonsense. But these are my people, though. These are the niggas I fuck with on a daily basis. So this is where I'm goin'. So Crescent City, Broadway Square, and Wooden Place, they're all one right behind the other on the same street. But here it is, we're young and dumb and we're beefing with each other. I'm beefing with these [other] niggas because they stay on Belfort and they come around our park sayin' "y'all niggas find somewhere else to go play basketball." (Interview with the author, April 2012)

Adrian's recollection highlights the territorialism present in the streets. While he lived in a single family home, Adrian's 'hood, or his primary social spots, was one of the many apartment complexes within TABB City. Nearby Dow Park, which sits at the intersection of Broadway and Rockhill Road, was a popular staging ground for street kids in the area. These youths frequented the park to play, but also to display markers of territorial identity such as hand signs and clothing. Residents of apartment complexes such as Crescent City, Broadway Square, and Wooden Place came to the park as collectives seeking to enact territorial dominance. Seizing the "neutral" basketball court meant a gain in status for their particular complex.

Big Be of the Bloc Boyz Click recalls the territorial confrontation between his native Cloverland and the adjacent Hillwood neighborhood: "I remember … when you couldn't come from Hillwood across the field without a fight. And Hillwood is the neighborhood back here [due south]. There are new houses right there right now, but before the new houses, there was just a field. And when I was a little fella, it was understood that when they come it's a fight. So you got everybody coming from the different sides to fight right there [at the field] because it's territorial" (interview with the author, April 2012).

Big Be reinforces the notion that violence is a core component of territorial behavior. Encroaching into foreign or unfamiliar territories can be treacherous, and this is true even for individuals who are unoriented and uninterested in territoriality. His following comments suggests that, sometimes, bonding within your 'hood is a practicality:

> Let's just say, you got this one particular apartment complex, it's only one apartment complex, but there's three others out here battlin.' So, when I was out there on Spice Lane, and this is elementary school, you understand. Kids, real kids. So, we walkin' down the street, I got to pass three apartment complexes that we supposedly battlin', or got beef with, before I make it to my elementary school. So that first ass whoopin' is going to teach you, "Man I got to walk with the rest of 'em." Everybody take an independent ass whoopin' or something happen to somebody you cut for or something like that. You gonna be like "Fuck that, we finna ride." (Interview with the author, April 2012)

Territoriality can be a necessity. The 'hood is a space where youths are actively bonding together and forming a variety of social groups, some related to the 'hood, but others emerging from other areas of shared interest. All of these groups are seeking respect, most often through the threat of violence. This can be a harrowing space for the unaffiliated. Being a loner or "one deep" as it's called in the streets can mean vulnerability to "independent ass whoopins." There's safety in numbers, and it is beneficial to bond with those with whom you have the most in common. Place becomes a popular bonding-agent, because it is immediate, tangible, and transparent. In short, for Big Be and others, territoriality is a direct response to the dangers of isolation within the inner city.

In the following remarks concerning the impetus behind a mid-1990s conflict between the Northside and Southside, Lil Raskull explicitly illuminated to me the process and impact of "reppin' your 'hood":

> The two roughest areas in Houston are South Park and Fifth Ward. If you're on the Northside, its undisputable that Fifth Ward is the hardest. If you're on the Southside its undisputable that South Park is the hardest. It was a territorial thing. It was a rivalry back then. It was testosterone. Dudes were tryin' to be hard. It was about who houses the roughest guys. Who has the toughest gangsters? The South or the North? Which side was the biggest ballers? Who's getting the most money in the dope game? The North or the South? That's what fueled the rivalry. (Interview with the author, 2012)

Raskull suggests that tension swelled and eventually erupted because, in his words, "dudes were tryin' to be hard." Individuals who sought the respect that came with being from the roughest 'hood fueled the competition between the two sides of town. It was a discursive game of one-upmanship. People from both sides created nefarious mythologies for their 'hoods by proactively calling attention to the street activity within them. As they increased the social respect for their 'hoods, they strengthened their personal status within the streets of Houston.

Over the course of one hundred and fifty years, Black Houstonians have taken their segregated neighborhoods, whose genesis lay in racist political practice, and converted them into culturally self-sufficient and autonomous spaces to affirm their identities and experiences. This remained true even as external socioeconomic forces ruptured the very core of these spaces, turning them into areas of concentrated poverty and unemployment. Even the streets, a byproduct of these forces defined by high rates of violence and assorted criminality, is a space of rich cultural activity. The language, the clothing, slabs, and lean have reverberated outside of the streets' abstract bounds, influencing both the 'hood and mainstream Houston society.

The streets' most prominent cultural contribution is the hyperlocal nature of Houston's hip hop identity. Local hip hop music is known for its unflinching commitment to reflecting local realities. This is due, in large part, to literal and performative engagement with the local streets. In the following section, I will discuss the role of the streets in the indigenization of Houston hip hop music and identity. In other words, I will examine how the streets, through the territorial practices of its inhabitants, turned "hip hop in Houston" into "Houston hip hop."

INDIGENIZATION OF HIP HOP IN HOUSTON STREETS

Houston had a thriving and impactful scene prior to the emergence of screw. Like other non–New York regional scenes, Houston's genesis began around the time of the South Bronx hip hop culture's commercialization, somewhere between the late 1970s and early 1980s, when records such as the Sugar Hill Gang's "Rapper's Delight," the Funky Four Plus One More's "Rappin' and Rockin' the House," and Kurtis Blow's "The Breaks" were released. Deejays spun these records during parties hosted by early Houston emcees Captain Jack and Wickett Crickett in clubs like the Fresh Connection on the Northside and Blue Ice on the Southside.

Local youth and young adults became captivated by hip hop almost overnight. Battling—informal or formal competition between emcees—was particularly popular. South Park legend and horrorcore pioneer Ganxsta NIP recalled battling during lunch periods at Jesse H. Jones High School in South Park:

> We used to have lunchtime battles. People from other schools would come to our school during lunchtime. Their friends would put money on them, and my homies would put money on me. And back then, it wasn't real lyrical; we were more direct. ... And I used to blow cats. Somebody might have $250 up on me, and there would be $250 up on the other cat. And at that particular time, I was broke. I'm just keeping it real. So by the time I took the other dude's $250, my partners would break me off $100 and I'm good. (Interview with the author, June 2012)

Similar battles occurred in parks and other spaces where Black youth congregated and in the form of emcee contests hosted by area clubs. The Rhinestone Wrangler, owned by legendary local club owner Ray Barnett, staged a weekly emcee contest that became a training ground for Houston's most treasured artists, including Willie D of the Geto Boys and South Park rapper K-Rino, who is now widely considered the godfather of Houston hip hop. The emcee battles were key aspects of the Rhinestone Wrangler's hip hop programming, which included parties helmed by deejays RP Cola and Steve Fornier.

Houston's earliest hip hop records reflected strong influences from and lyrical hints to local experience. In 1985, the LA Rapper released "McGregor Park," an ode to the iconic South Park social space. "McGregor Park" used an electro-funk–based soundscape, but featured lyrics that detailed the social life of Southside youth during the mid-1980s, including the car parties that were often held on park grounds. While the lyrics contain an aspect of local identity, the electro-hop–based sounds and the rapper's West Coast–identified moniker compromise the indigenousness of the record. In a similar vein was the Ghetto Boys' "Car Freaks" (1986), a song journalist Roni Sarig describes as "a bass-inspired track about girls more interested in a guy's car than in the guy himself" (2007, 42). While the song is grounded in the misogynistic gold-digger archetype, the Ghetto Boys members Sire Jukebox, Raheem, and K9 do highlight the centrality of car culture within local Black culture. While its lyrics hinted at local identity, the production and vocal style reflected a strong New York influence, and particularly seemed inspired by the commercially popular styles of Whodini and UTFO.

Spurred on by the popularity of the local hip hop club scene, as well as the commercial success of hip hop records around the country, local luxury-car dealer James "J. Prince" Smith created Rap-A-Lot Records, the city's first dedicated hip hop label, in 1985. The label's early roster included several New York transplants. Rick Royal, of the group Royal Flush, had grown up in New Jersey and had spent time in California before moving to Houston in the early 1980s. The Def IV featured members from Brooklyn and Chicago. The group's deejay, DJ Vicious Lee, along with Ready Red, helped craft Rap-A-Lot's early sound. Smith also restructured the Ghetto Boys, replacing members Raheem and K9 with DJ Ready Red, Prince Johnny C, and dancer Lil Billy, all of whom had East Coast origins. Many of these artists moved to Houston as teens in the 1980s as part of a larger trend in which Black Americans moved southward. These East Coast transplants brought their regional musical sensibilities with them and infused them into their new musical productions (Sarig 2007, xvii). As a result, Rap-A-Lot Records' earliest releases featured East Coast–influenced soundscapes and lyrical styles.

In the wake of *Making Trouble*'s success, Prince Johnny C and Jukebox quit the Geto Boys over artistic differences. Wanting to build upon the group's success, Lil J replaced the departed members with two emcees from opposite sides of Houston: Willie D from Fifth Ward and Scarface from South Park. Along with the retained DJ Ready Red and the hypeman-turned-emcee Bushwick Bill, they became known as the Geto Boys. This iteration of the group differed widely from its predecessors. Gone were the up-tempo dance tracks and occasional high-spirited, novelty numbers. These Geto Boys embraced the gangsta style, popularized by West Coast gangsta-rap acts like Ice-T and N.W.A. and taking over hip hop airwaves nationwide. Anthropologist Ali Colleen Neff states that the Geto Boys "used West Coast gangsta scripts to discuss their experience with southern poverty" (2011, 156). Roni Sarig expounds on her claim: "While locals pride themselves on the Geto Boys being among rap's original gangstas—arriving earlier or simultaneous with N.W.A.—evidence suggests that Willie D and his Rap-A-Lot cohorts were intimately familiar with N.W.A. and earlier L.A. rappers like Ice-T before their own gangsta stance had fully formed. Lyricists Scarface and Willie D appropriated West Coast gangsta tales into narratives that reflected local experience" (2007, 45). The group's signature song, "Mind Playin Tricks" (1991), a haunting journey into the psychological depths of street life, features some markers of locality. The song's melody contains a sample of soul-singer Isaac Hayes's "Hung Up on My Baby," an example of the Southern soul sound popular among Houston audiences at that time. Willie D's and Scarface's relaxed vocals and Southern drawls broke from hip hop's sonic convention. Nevertheless, "Mind Playin' Tricks" was a Southern take on a West Coast aesthetic, not a homegrown sound.

I would be remiss not to highlight contributions of the South Park Coalition, a loose collective that reflects the stylistic diversity of Houston's scene of the late 1980s and early 1990s. Since its formation in 1987, it has been a crew consisting of nearly sixty solo artists, groups, and producers from the Houston area (Lynch 2009, 447). Its founder and leader, K-Rino, is known for his intricate battle-oriented lyricism and commonly considered the godfather of Houston rap. The aforementioned Ganxsta NIP is known as one of the earliest "horrorcore" rappers, using lyrical themes and images grounded in horror aesthetics. Another South Park neighborhood group, The Terrorists, took Public Enemy–styled, conscious rap to new levels on their Rap-A-Lot releases in the early 1990s. Street Military produced a psychedelic form of gangsta rap and became the earliest Houston group to release an album on a non-Houston–based record label, Wild Pitch Records. Point Blank, from South Park by way of Chicago, is a quintessential Houston gangsta rapper.

While Houston's early hip hop history was certainly full of valuable contributions to the national hip hop landscape, it lacked the indigenously formed and unprecedented styles that made Los Angeles an important hip hop center in the late 1980s. Early Houston artists appropriated styles from the east and west coasts, inscribing them with occasional references to local experience, but stopping short of creating a musical form that can be uniquely identified with the city.

FROM HOUSTON TO SCREWSTON

By the early 1990s, Houston had an active hip hop scene, which featured a prominent label in Rap-A-Lot Records, a hip hop–based radio station at 97.9 FM, and countless artists; it lacked, however, a native sound. Besides casual references to local sites or situations in the lyrics, there was little to distinguish Houston's rap acts from New York and Los Angeles rappers who were dominating radio and television at that time.

In the early 1990s, the organic development of the screw sound gave Houston a distinctly local hip hop identity. The screwed-and-chopped deejay technique is the central component of the screw sound, and it involves two separate practices: screwing and chopping. To screw, deejays slow the tempo of a record between 30 and 50 percent, creating a muddy, bass-heavy sound, accompanied by haunting vocals. *Chopping* is a localism for the common deejay practice of repeating certain words or phrases in a song, creating a percussive effect. The combination of these practices creates a psychedelic and atmospheric hip hop sound. Local producers have turned the screwed-and-chopped technique into a dragging, trippy, and bass-heavy production style. In addition, screw-based rappers commonly perform in a smooth, melodious manner, which accentuates the musical accompaniment. Their lyrics are grounded in the acute particulars of Houston street life. Screw lyrics are hyperlocal, as artists make explicit references to the people, places, and activities that make up the Houston landscape.

Several myths about the origins of the screw style circulate within the Houston hip hop community. One story attributes its origins to DJ Darryl Scott, the legendary Southside deejay whose R&B and funk-filled mixtapes were popular within the Southside from the mid- to the late 1980s. Scott recalls joking around by playing 45-rpm records at 33-rpm speed to slow down music as early as the late 1970s. He slowed three or four songs on a few personal mixes that he made for two Southside customers in the late 1980s. While acknowledging his early forays into slowed music, he credits his protégé, DJ Michael Price, with pioneering the style. According to Scott, during a late-1980s party on Calumet Street in Third Ward, Price was playing a Darryl Scott mixtape through a boom box when the box's batteries began to drain. This resulted in slowed output from the speakers. The sluggish sounds captivated that night's audience and inspired Price to investigate the style further. Price then rigged his boombox to produce slowed output on full batteries by pressing a screw against the tape motor—which, for Scott, is how the style became known as screw in the first place. Price proceeded to deejay parties and produce mixtapes with slowed sounds until he was stabbed to death in 1993.

Most Houstonians, however, attribute the screwed style to the late DJ Screw, the Southside deejay whose legend continues to dominate the local scene. DJ Screw was born Robert Earl Davis Jr., in Smithville, Texas, a small town about 40 miles southeast of Austin. After seeing the b-boy film *Breakin'* in 1984, he became enamored with hip hop culture and was particularly attracted to deejaying. He first used his mother's consumer turntable to mix and scratch her blues recordings and then rigged up his own system. According to his childhood friend Shorty Mac, "Screw had a jam box and he hooked up two turntables to it and made a fader out of the radio tuner so he could deejay" (Hall 2001). Shorty Mac gave Robert Earl his deejay moniker, DJ Screw, because he used a screw to destroy records he did not like. After a brief stay in California, young Screw moved to Houston, where his father was working as a truck driver and was living in South Park's Quail Meadow Apartments. Screw honed his skills for several years before turning professional in the late 1980s. Lacking adequate equipment, he partnered with another young Southside disk jockey, DJ Chill, and the two pooled their resources.

The two burgeoning deejays began to play teenage clubs and parties around the Southside.

There are also conflicting stories about what inspired DJ Screw to decelerate the tempo of the records he spun. Darryl Scott argues that DJ Screw embraced the sound after partnering with Michael Price. The two produced slowed-down mixtapes and brought them to Scott for his assessment. Screw's friend and initial manager, Charles Washington, tells a different story. He recalls a night in 1989 when DJ Screw was mixing for his friends. His arm accidentally hit the turntable's pitch control knob, which slowed the music down. Screw liked the way it sounded, as did his associates, who offered him $10 for slowed-down tapes. For Washington, the Screw style was born that night (Hall 2001).

Regardless of its origin, DJ Screw was the chief innovator and popularizer of the slowed hip hop music. In 1990, he began selling personalized slow mixes to Southside residents for $10. Customers would give him a list of twenty hip hop songs, which he would mix together using a variety of deejay practices, including his trademark chopping. He would then use a four-track recorder to slow down the mixes and transfer them to 90-minute Maxell cassettes. These early tapes primarily featured local artists such

Figure 2. DJ Screw mural inside of Action Smoke Shop in Houston, Texas. Photo by author.

as Underground Kingz (UGK), Geto Boys, and Street Military, along with West Coast gangsta artists like Tupac and Screw's personal favorite artist, C-Bo. Screw also mixed in East Coast artists such as Nas and the Notorious B.I.G., along with old-school R&B for good measure.

As the tapes grew in popularity, Screw began to invite friends and customers to "rep their 'hoods" on his mixtapes. These vocal performances came in the form of mixtape intros, shoutouts, and impromptu rap performances, known within hip hop culture as freestyles. These freestyles were completely extemporaneous vocal performances, devoid of prior preparation. The earliest screwtape freestylers did not dream of becoming professional rap artists; they were individuals who saw an opportunity to rep themselves and their 'hoods.

Driven by territorial urges, these freestylers came from all over the Southside to make tapes with DJ Screw. C-Note, considered the first person to freestyle on a screwtape, was from Cloverland, Mike D was from Third Ward, and Fat Pat and Lil Keke represented different regions of South Park. In addition to functioning as a site of musical production, Screw's house became a valued recreational site within the streets. Speaking as part of a panel during the University of Houston's 2012 Awwready! Houston Hip Hop Conference, Lil Keke labeled DJ Screw's house "a campground for different neighborhoods" and added, "It was a neighborhood thang. It went from a singled-out thing and then it became about Third Ward, Botany, Herschelwood, and Fourth Ward and South Park and everything. And Screw, he was like the captain of all those neighborhoods."

Lil Keke's comments illuminate DJ Screw's role as a community mediator within the Southside. The musical activity that he facilitated within his home allowed territorially fueled competition to be negotiated without the specter of the violence that often springs from street interactions. By producing screwtapes, individual street actors from disparate communities were able to fellowship within the context of musical performance.

This loose-knit collective of freestylers eventually united and became known as the Screwed Up Click (S.U.C.). Its rapping members have included Fat Pat (1970–1998), Big Hawk (1969–2006), Lil Keke, Lil Randy, E.S.G., Big Pokey, Mike D, Big Moe (1974–2007), Mr. 3-2 (1973–2016), Lil O, Stick 1, Clay Doe, Big Steve (1974–1999), Big Demo, Macc Grace (1973–2017), Wood, Big Mello (1968–2017), Yungstar, Trae tha Truth, Lil Flip, Z-Ro, and the Botany

Boyz (C-Note, Will Lean, D-Red, BG Duke), along with dozens of others. The S.U.C. included a host of nonrapping members, such as Corey Blount, Pat Lemon, and Trevie Trell, important street figures within the Southside. DJ Screw helmed the entire assemblage.

A DJ Screw recording session was a Southside social event. Screwed Up Click member E.S.G. describes the common setting: "You come in the big room, you know what I'm sayin'. You chillin' with your partners. ... Everybody sittin' around talkin' and chillin', listenin' to Screw make a tape. You got your list down. Taking your turn with your partners. Hollerin' out your 'hood, or even freestylin'. Or doin' whatever you want to do" (interview with the author, 2012). In this commentary, E.S.G. portrays Screw's recording sessions as big house parties. Screw's turntable performances facilitated the recreational interaction among those present, which included members of the Screwed Up Click along with their associates. In many cases, these extramusical interactions were captured on tape, making them part of the musical product. Along with freestyles and Screw's turntable virtuosity, a screwtape contains a significant amount of background chatter, laughing, sounds of drinks being poured, and other elements that mark a party atmosphere. The line between artist and audience is blurred. The musical product includes all persons present during the recording session, whether self-defined rappers or not.

Recording was a relatively unstructured and informal process for the Screwed Up Click. Member Lil Randy told me that these sessions would last several hours, sometimes beginning in the mid-evening and not ending until the next morning. He thus elucidates, "Screw would just turn the turntables on, press record, and that's what it is. He do his thang. We just sit back and listen to it. If somebody would be feelin' the beat, they'd be like 'Hey Screw, let me wreck off that.' Or Screw would put on a beat and be like 'Hey man you feelin' this?' Then you'd freestyle off of it, or you didn't" (interview with the author, 2012). Lil Randy describes a process whereby musical activity organically emerged out of social interaction. In the midst of drinking, smoking, and general fraternizing, Screwed Up Click rappers randomly and intermittingly performed extemporaneous rapped verses. So, while it was the musical performance that set the context for the event, screwtape performances were subsumed within and subordinate to the larger social event.

DJ Screw's *No Drank* (1995) offers insight into the screwtape recording process. Produced in 1995, *No Drank* stands as one of the most prized tapes within the Houston hip hop community because of its iconic freestyles from Fat Pat and Lil Keke, along with fellow Screwed Up Click members Boo and Dave. The tape opens with an introduction from Fat Pat, whose vocals document the atmosphere: "It's goin' down. Don't let them knock you off your game. [Speaking away from the mic.] You know what? Everybody be sayin' that. Ah man, he done made an ass of himself. He said something playa, but he's an ass man. [Assorted laughter, then Fat Pat speaks back into the mic.] Nah, I'm just playin' with y'all, man. I'm just playin' with you, dog. What's up Bubba-love!"

The audio captures Fat Pat, mid-sentence, speaking to the guests at DJ Screw's house. He then turns away from the microphone to respond to inaudible comments and proceeds to tease the source of these comments, which provokes laughter all around. The setting becomes clearer with Fat Pat's follow-up:

> Yeah, what's up? What you talkin' 'bout? What's happenin'? I'm in the house. It's that Fat Pat with that Dave and that Boo. And that Keke and Screw. Nigga, what? We got that Chris and that Blount in the house. What's up, playboy, what's your name? We got Darryl in the house with the two little mamas looking good in the back, wearin' black. Man, cuz, it's goin' down. It's really goin' down, H-Town, Texas. What's up. You know we real. It's real on this side. We wreckin', so what you talkin' 'bout? So what you talkin' 'bout?

Here, Fat Pat acknowledges and introduces the parties in attendance for the recording session. This includes Screwed Up Click members Dave, Boo, Lil Keke, and Screw, who perform on the tape. He recognizes nonrapping S.U.C. members Chris and Corey Blount, as well as an unfamiliar man named Darryl, who is accompanied by two unnamed women. At this point, Fat Pat moves seamlessly into a freestyle that he performs with Lil Keke, Boo, and Dave over an instrumental provided by Screw. Such nonrapped dialogue continues throughout the tape and seems to structure the rap performances.

The communal nature of the screwtape production is not unique to the Screwed Up Click. This is a common process within the African American musical tradition. Historically, Black music has been collectively created within social contexts. As ethnomusicologist Portia Maultsby notes, "The fundamental concept that governs music performance in African and

African-derived cultures is that music-making is a participatory group activity that serves to unite black people into a cohesive group for a common purpose" (2005, 329). This Africanism is evident in other African American musical cultures, whether sacred or secular. Gospel music, in church settings, involves the active participation of audience members who assist vocalists through body percussion. Hip hop in its precommercial phase was produced within block-party and house-party contexts. Music making, for African Americans, has been rooted in collective practice and serves a common purpose (Brown 2015). In Houston, that purpose was to celebrate place and to communicate important messages across the community.

THE SCREWTAPE AS COMMUNITY RADIO

Among Houston Southsiders, DJ Screw's mixtapes functioned as a type of documentation and communication medium for Southside street life. "Screwtapes were like a 'hood radio," Lil Randy of the Screwed Up Click told me: "The screwtapes was a major voice in the 'hood." On the tapes, Lil Randy and his fellow S.U.C. members offered musical messages that detailed the important people, places, events, practices, and attitudes relevant to Southside life. They rapped about wearing bald fades, the signature haircut of the Southside streets.

There were many birthday tapes. The *June 27* tape recording that was made in celebration of S.U.C. member Demo's birthday is among the most venerated tapes for its 37-minute-long group freestyle. Fat Pat's last tape appearance was on *It's All Good* (1997), made in celebration of his twenty-seventh birthday. *Leanin' on a Switch* and *Headed to the League* commemorated S.U.C. member Big Pokey getting switches on his vehicle and his National Football League tryout respectively. *9 Months Later (1996)* was made for S.U.C. member Torie to mark the recent birth of her baby. S.U.C. member Skinny Shaun freestyled on *Off Parole*, a tape made to honor his return to the streets after five years of incarceration. *Graduation 99* marks S.U.C. member D-Drew's high-school graduation. According to legend, D-Drew's mother prohibited him from rapping on a screwtape until he finished high school; for him, the tape represented the transition from boyhood to manhood and reflected a new status within the S.U.C. He died in 2008, becoming one of the many fallen members of the Screwed Up Click. Many memorial mixtapes were produced, including ones for S.U.C. members Trevie Trell, Pat Lemon, and multiples for Fat Pat.

Syrup, the codeine-based drug concoction popular within the Southside streets, complements the hazy, slow-tempo soundscape of the screwtapes. S.U.C. rappers celebrated the drug in countless freestyles. The following Fat Pat verse, from DJ Screw's *Let's Call Up on Drank*, represents the manner in which S.U.C. members extolled their fondness for syrup:

> Shit, for life, that's me, P-A-T
> Nigga always drank the codeine
> Always wanna lean

Syrup inspired many screwtape titles, including *Whole Sippin Codeine, Syrup & Soda, Codeine Fiend,* and *On a Pint. No Drank* was inspired by a codeine shortage on the Southside. The Screwed Up Click rapped about lean so frequently that many listeners saw it as the illicit counterpart of the music. "When Screw start screwing the music down, it was the perfect soundtrack to syrup," said Justice Allah (interview with the author, January 2012). DJ Screw downplayed the association. In a 1999 interview with *Murder Dog* magazine, Screw said "Cause I play my music slow, people think you gotta get high, get fucked up, do drugs, just to listen to my music. It ain't like that at all" (Bray 1999). Nevertheless, screw music raised the drug's profile within the Southside streets. Studies (Elwood 2001, Peters et al. 2003) have suggested that the Screwed Up Click's promotion of syrup on screwtapes caused usage of the drug to reach epidemic levels by the early 2000s.

Like syrup, slab also played a central role in Screwed Up Click subject matter. Rappers commonly mentioned the practice in their verses, and it inspired the titles of several tapes, including *Leanin' On a Switch, Popped Up Sittin' Low,* and *Sittin' Sideways.* Further, the Screwed Up Click's music helped make red the most relevant slab color on the Southside. According to Lil Randy:

> Back in the days before Screw, you kind of represented yourself with your car. The way your car was fixed up, that represented you. Honestly, when Screw came about, the whole Southside was painting their cars red. You heard Corey Blount talkin' about red. You heard Pat Lemmon talkin about red. You heard, ya know, me and my brother Ron-O and Randy talkin' about red. That was a voice for the 'hood. So it's like kids listening to the

radio: they're gonna go by what they hear. So these screwtapes were getting so popular, it was like the 'hood radio. That's what made the whole Southside paint their cars red. (Interview with the author, April 2012)

Lil Randy explicitly attributes the popularity of red slabs in the Southside to the music of the Screwed Up Click. Before the emergence of screwtapes, slabs expressed individual identity. Lil Randy, for example, notes that he painted his first slabs red because it had long been his favorite color. A finished slab was product of individual ingenuity with little to no communal motivations. After hearing Screwed Up Click members Pat Lemmon, Corey Blount, Randy, and his brother Ron-O talk about red slabs on screwtapes, Southsiders began painting their cars red as a grand display of their newly developed collective identity.

"Reppin' the 'hood" was a prominent aspect of the Screwed Up Click's freestyle performances. Lil Keke, Fat Pat, Big Pokey, and other members of the collective vociferously "repped for their 'hoods" by referencing neighborhood names and citing the street activity that operated within their bounds. In addition, many personal tapes were named after the solicitor's neighborhood. For example, *Cloverland* (1994) was a personal tape made for Cloverland native and Botany Boyz member BG Gator. Similarly, *Yellowstone Texas* (1995) was a tape made for Big Pokey, who represented Yellowstone, a small neighborhood positioned between Third Ward and Sunnyside. *Herschelwood* (1994) was a tape made by the Herschelwood Hardheadz, an offshoot group of the Screwed Up Click led by Lil Keke from the Herschelwood section of South Park.

While specific neighborhoods were commonly cited, rappers were more likely to reference the larger Southside collective. The Screwed Up Click boldly celebrated the Southside at every turn. Lil Randy, during his freestyle on DJ Screw's *Done Deal*, proudly raps, "I'm from the Southside and we known for straight wreckin.'" *Southside Riders*, *Southside Holdin*, *Southside's Most Wanted*, and *Worldwide Southside* are among numerous screwtapes that include references to the Southside in their titles.

For members of the Screwed Up Click, who came from different neighborhoods and had different backgrounds, Southside identity was a point of unity. Whereas the sociomusical activity at DJ Screw's house facilitated the destruction of territorial barriers among members of the S.U.C., shouting

"Southside" on screwtapes did the same for their multineighborhood fan base. "The screwtapes brought the Southside together," says Lil Randy. "When we started screaming Southside, [other Southside] people started shouting Southside on a massive level" (interview with the author, 2012).

"Houston realized that DJ Screw gave Houston its identity in hip hop. The slowed down music, which we call Screw music, is Houston's identity in hip hop," Lil Randy once enthusiastically expressed to me. Like Compton and Miami before it, Houston now had a fusion of sounds, verbal styles, and lyrical content that would distinguish it from other regional centers of hip hop production. The Screwed Up Click accomplished this by inscribing their music with the social realities of the Southside streets. Their art indexed and immortalized the experiences of folks like OG Scott and transformed them into a hyperlocal aesthetic. As Screw fan and disciple Big Be told me: "You can point to every particular characteristic of Houston right now and I guarantee you, it was on those tapes. From the drugs to ... I remember at one point in time, all I liked was yellow bones because I wanted a 'yellow bone on the side, sittin' sideways.' For real though. Everything that we have that we can call our own was glorified and magnified on those tapes" (interview with the author, 2012).

The music affirmed and influenced the youngsters like Big Be who were listening to the tapes in their rides and Walkmans. Through DJ Screw and Screwed Up Click, screw music, slabs, lean, and reppin' the 'hood coalesced into a cultural identity that artists, both local and non-local, continue to engage with in their music today.

3

STILL TIPPIN'

From the slabs to the music, man. I just congratulate Houston
for creating an imprint that's here to stay.

—Big Love

Big Love is beaming with pride as he speaks to me from his home in Houston. With his healthy grey beard betraying his otherwise youthful look, he embraces his role as a Houston hip hop griot of sorts, always willing to spread knowledge about the history and culture. "I'm one of those old guys with all the stories you know, and you don't get them until you sit him down and let him dust off and think about them. So, anytime man, I'm here for you" (interview with the author, 2021).

Big Love is very much an elder statesman within the Houston hip hop scene, having contributed to foundations of his local sound with 1997's *Representin' Real*. Recorded when he was only two years removed from high school, the rapper sounded well beyond his age as he spoke of both the harsh realities and pleasures of life in Houston's Northside Studewood neighborhood. These tales were imaginings pulled from his life but also the lives of his older brothers and friends who were deep in the streets. The music was his way of getting away from that life. "I was seeing both sides of the drug game and hip hop, for me, was a way of getting away from these decisions."

Representing Real dropped as Houston's local hip hop identity was starting to form, and the music contains frequent references to screw music, lean, and slab. The record was regionally successful and allowed Big Love to spread the "Houston sound" all over the South. "We were just trying to get the music and represent Houston to the fullest we could," he humbly notes. Alongside recordings from the Screwed Up Click and Swishahouse, Big Love's *Representin' Real* helped crystallize Houston's hip hop identity in the local and national imagination. The album's impact continues to be felt among younger street-based artists. I remember EDF urging me to listen to the album. "It defines everything about this Houston culture," he told me.

Since *Representin' Real*, Big Love has been a bit of a renaissance man, branching out into other industries like real estate and logistics. Houston hip hop remains a central part of his professional life. He's released several projects through his own independent label, Candy Sto' Productions, and mentors younger artists. "Getting older, man, as I learned stuff, I try to pass it on to the younger guys," he says. "They know I'm always game to give them knowledge."

Alongside the music, Big Love spends much of his time offering his knowledge on another core element of Houston hip hop heritage—slabs. Featuring candy paint, booming sound systems, and extended cone-shaped rims, slab has been a part of Black Houston's visual and sonic landscape since the mid-1980s. Big Love is a slab customizer, a community artisan who helps novice riders and veterans create their cars. "Yeah man, you basically drop your car off at a shop or a guy who does customization like me and you know, tell us your dreams." It certainly can be a lucrative business, since building a slab can cost several thousand dollars. However, for Big Love, it is about more than business. It's cultural preservation. "It's the culture, man. It's Houston. It's us. We did it. I'm just pleased to be a part of something that you can see nationwide and know that you were originally one of the guys who were toying around with this sound and these cars and this great city."

In Houston, slab culture and hip-hop music go hand-in-hand, having been organically bonded during the early years of both practices, another product of the relationship between people and place. The inseparable connection between slab and local hip hop music has had far-reaching implications for both hip hop culture and its Black community of origin. Slabs were a catalyst in the emergence of Houston hip hop's unique identity in the early 1990s and soon after were central to a violent community conflict. It also helped mainstream the scene in the first decade of the 2000s, defining Houston hip hop heritage both within and outside of town.

WHaT IS a SLaB?

Slab is a unique vernacular car practice that centers on transforming older-model luxury sedans into elaborate and almost futuristic-looking socio-musical machines. According to E.S.G., "In the beginning time, more than likely, it was an old-school car. You know what I'm sayin'. It couldn't be an old Datsun, Nissan. It had to be big, ya know. It didn't have to be just Cadillac. It could've been Buicks. You know what I'm talkin' 'bout. It could've been different brands of cars. It could've been Ford or anything. But it had to be kind of big" (interview with the author, 2012). The tradition privileges large American luxury cars produced by makers such as Cadillac, Lincoln, Mercury, and Oldsmobile as well as larger lines produced by Chevrolet and Ford. At the core of slab culture is the owner's desire to be recognized, to make his presence felt within his social group. Therefore, larger cars are more desired because they bring more attention to the owner. As Daunte from the Bloc Boyz notes, slab bodies are preferably something "big, long, and wide that will hog the road" (interview with the author, 2012). "Old-school" also has a temporal dimension in this context. The slab aesthetic also values older cars, those produced from the 1970s to the 1990s. These models were bigger and boxier and featured standard features that became core parts of the slab aesthetic.

The term "slab" refers to the slabs of concrete that make up a street or paved road. It emerged in the early days of the culture, when the act of driving the modified car was known as "hitting the slab." Others suggest that the term comes from the fact that all the modifications make the car sit lower, closer

Figure 3. Teal slabs at Slab Holiday in Galveston, Texas, on May 19, 2012. Photo by author.

Figure 4. Front end of a slab at Slab Holiday in Galveston, Texas, on May 19, 2012. Photo by author.

to the concrete slabs of the street. Today, slab also is expressed in acronym form to mean "Slow, Loud, And Bangin."

Most cars feature multi-layered iridescent paint jobs, known as "candy paint," that give them a wet look when hit by light. Interiors include leather seats as well as woodgrain steering wheel and dashboards. The chrome grill and "woman," or hood ornament, structures the front end. The centerpiece of the back end is the "5th wheel," a rim or wheel that is cut in half and enclosed in a fiberglass casing. It sits in a "bumper kit" that allows it to be attached to the trunk. Actuators allow slab riders to remotely raise or "pop" their trunks to reveal the elaborate, neon LED displays positioned inside. Featuring references to neighborhoods, social groups, and fallen friends, these trunk displays allow slab riders to communicate explicit messages to those within and outside of their communities.

The most important distinguishing aesthetic component of a slab, what separates this from other urban car cultures, are the rims, called "swangas" (also called "elbows"). Swangas refer to two styles of rim that Crager Wheel Company produced for Cadillac models in the early 1980s: the "83s" and the "84s." The first version of the rim, the original 83s, were thirty-spoke chrome rims produced between 1979 and 1983. In 1984, the rim was modified. The center hub was moved further out, meaning the spokes poked out more. These "84s" also featured a reduced lip and more space between the outer ten spokes, as well as some modifications to the inner twenty spokes. Because of safety issues, the original 84s were only produced for one year (1984), which meant there were very few of them available in later years. Naturally, this made the 84s more valued and more valuable than the 83s. Vogues, tires marked by their distinctive whitewall and yellow stripe, are a core slab component and common to other car culture in the American south.

Slab is also a musical practice. Cars feature explosive, bass-heavy stereo systems that are powered by multiple batteries. The goal is the make the trunk rattle, so others can see, hear, and feel your presence. This practice goes beyond aesthetics, revealing the important role of hip hop and other forms of Black music within the lives of its practitioners. "When you play your music in your slab, it's displaying who you are or what type of mood you're in," conveys slab rider, customizer, and documentarian Meyagi (interview with the author, 2014).

Slabs do not come pre-packaged. They are not mass-produced. You cannot stop by a dealership and say, "Hey, I want a slab." A car is transformed into a

Figure 5. Back end of a slab at Slab Holiday in Galveston, Texas, on May 19, 2012. Photo by author.

slab. "A true slab is something you build from the ground up and you put your heart and soul into it," Meyagi explained to me (interview with the author, 2014). Big Love expresses a similar sentiment. "You get to be Frankenstein, you know," he says. "You find the model car you want; you get your ideas what color paint you want, how you want to do your interior, how you want to do your trunk, and it's just the whole creative process and when you're done you see what you create is like, man, look at my candy toy" (interview with the author, 2021). Traditionally, slab riders purchase their cars when they are in a more modest state, called "hoopties," and slowly convert them into elaborate slabs. A slab is built from the inside out, starting with the engine, with the rider carefully choosing every component part. This process can take years and cost several thousand. While slab riders often employ their own handiwork in the creation of their vehicles, they also use the services of community craftsmen like Todd "B.G." Porter or China Boy for the more intricate components. In this sense, like all folk arts, a finished slab is the result of both individual and communal development.

SLAB HISTORY AND MEANING

"The reason people wanted that rim was because that rim came on a Cadillac. It was a Cadillac rim," China Boy says about the emergence of swangas. "I was told that a Cadillac was originally designed by a Black man, so that's an African American's rim" (interview with the author, 2013). I could not substantiate China Boy's claim that a Black man invented the Cadillac. True or not, I was not surprised to hear this idea. Folklorist Patricia Turner writes that "products or places having strong symbolic potency for African Americans may inspire speculation that is then manifested as rumor or contemporary legend" (Turner 1993, 172). If you lived in a Southern city in the post-Civil Rights era, you know that Cadillacs occupy an important or almost spiritual place. They are ubiquitous. Long-bodied Eldorados and Wide-bodied Escalades glide down Black streets or stoically stand in Black driveways. Some folks like the regality of 1960s and '70s models. Others prefer the sleek but formidable models from the 1990s through 2000s. Every Cadillac has its place. They are transcendent and pole-breaking, popular along the spectrum from pimp to pastor.

Naturally, Cadillacs are the premier make within slab culture. It's the gold standard. Its cultural weight within slab and Black culture did not occur by happenstance. Slab culture reflects the longstanding role of luxury cars within Black culture, a position that has shifted across time, region, and class status. Slab and car culture reflect malleable Black desire for liberty, upward mobility, and both literacy and symbolic power.

Slab first emerged on the Houston streets of the 1980s but is part of a Black car continuum that can be traced back to the Great Depression. As the story goes, GM, the corporation that owns the Cadillac brand, was in bad financial shape like other entities during the Great Depression. To save the brand, company executive Nick Dreystadt burst into an executives' meeting and urged his colleagues to break longstanding policy by marketing to African Americans. Cadillac, like other automakers, refused to sell cars to Black people, feeling that such a practice would spurn the White consumer base. Despite this, Dreystadt noted that many of the cars brought in for service were owned by Black people. It seems that the small but growing Black middle class were paying White people to buy the cars for them. They were deeply connected to the prestige of the Cadillac and its function as a form of cultural capital, one that could symbolically lift them up out of racial and economic subjugation. As Margaret Myers and Sharon G. Dean write, "Cadillac was the only success symbol the affluent Negro could buy; he had no access to good housing, to luxury resorts, or to any other of the outward signs of worldly success" (Myers and Dean 2007, 160). Marketing and selling cars to the Black middle class allowed Cadillac to break even in 1934, staving off proposed liquidation.

By the mid-1950s, car culture had become a key way middle-class African Americans asserted their class identity and symbolically subverted racial domination. As historian Fon L. Gordon writes, "The private motorcar for black citizens provided a space to avoid and recuperate from Jim Crow assault. Motoring mobility was a political, social, and cultural tool and counter-narrative that enabled African Americans to elude racial restrictions and participate in Atlantic and American modernity" (2017, 524). The sheer ability to move about space was a liberatory practice. Coming from a legacy of physical restriction, the semi-open road signified their movement past the furthest reaches of social control (Wilkins 2021). According to sociologist Paul Gilroy, "histories of confinement and coerced labor must have given them additional receptivity to the pleasures of auto-autonomy as a means of escape, transcendence and even resistance" (2001, 84). Post-war Black and mainstream media reflected the power of car culture. In a 1949 *Ebony* magazine article titled "Why Blacks Drive Cadillacs," magazine founder John H. Johnson wrote that the Cadillac "is a sign of wealth and standing so to Negro Americans the Cadillac is an indication of ability to compete successfully with whites" (34). Blues and rock and roll records also indexed the impact of car culture within Black America. Luxury car brands were central characters in songs like Lightening Hopkins's "Big Car Blues," Chuck Berry's "Maybellene," and Ike Turner's "Rocket 88."

While car culture was ubiquitous in Black America, it did not come without critique. Soul singer William DeVaughn offers a clear rejection of car culture in his 1970 song "Be Thankful." DeVaughn wrote the original version of the song, "A Cadillac Don't Come Easy," when he was a government worker and part-time singer. He rewrote it and spent $900 of his own money to release it through Roxbury Records, and it went on to sell over a million copies. The lyrics offer a sharp repudiation of the prominence of car culture in Black America, taking explicit aim at the way it ties self-worth to materialism. "I was trying to create some lyrics that would help them keep their self-esteem," DeVaughn told the *Washington Post* in 1999 (Merida 1999). His thesis is most evident in the following lines:

> You may not drive a great big Cadillac,
> gangsta white walls and a TV antenna in the back,
> though you may not have a car at all,
> remember brothers and sisters, you can still stand tall

These lines are certainly memorable. However, it's the song's chorus that became part of Black musical consciousness in the 1970s and onward. "Diamond in the back, sunroof top, diggin' the scene with the gangsta lean" was a cultural zeitgeist thanks to DeVaughn's rhythmic crooning and the band's soulful accompaniment. The chorus undermined DeVaughn's anti-materialistic message and even became a car culture anthem. It became associated with what could be considered the most fully realized example of DeVaughn's critique—pimp culture. Professor and cultural critic Todd Boyd writes that "'Be Thankful for What You Got' helps to define the Super Fly '70s through its chill, weed-induced, pimped-out sound, and its evocation of images from the pimp life, in spite of the inherent critique in the lyrics" (Boyd 2007, 156). Whitewall tires, TV screens, and the "diamond in the back" were all components of the heavily and stylishly modified vehicles owned by pimps, a vernacular car practice that is commonly called the "pimp mobile."

Pimps have occupied their own cultural space within Black folk and popular culture. In *Pimping Fictions: African American Crime Literature and the Untold Story of Black Pulp Publishing*, Justin Gifford notes that pimps were represented in the literary works of Claude McKay, Ann Petrey, Ralph Ellison, and others (2013, 42). In the 1970s, the pimp's cultural significance rose as many young Black men, who were facing the increasingly desolate conditions of American inner cities, saw them as subversive cultural forces. As Eithne Quinn writes, "For young black men facing unemployment there were clear culture-building possibilities in exalting heroic hustlers—particularly the 'lifestylized' pimp—who repudiated mainstream and menial jobs and joblessness in favor of antiassimilationist pursuits that at least promised a viable means of income" (2001, 224). Much of this culture building happened through creative expression. Young Black men gravitated toward pimp literature written by Robert Beck, whose popular Iceberg Slim character Justin Gifford calls "a figure of heroic black masculinity whose verbal style and posture of criminal cool could offer tactile challenges to white racism" (2013, 42). In his 2012 memoir, rapper Ice-T recalls memorizing and reciting sections of Beck's book when he was in high school, and it was the inspiration behind his rap moniker. It must be said that the pimp's cultural prominence, and young Black men's related aspirational imaginings, came at the expense of Black women. Pimping is a deeply misogynistic capitalist enterprise.

According to notable pimp and Snoop Dogg affiliate Bishop Don Magic Juan, "a pimp is judged by his flash, his Cadillac, his house, his jewelry, his clothes."[1] Customized cars were core components of a pimp's image and "workflow." Reflecting the highly misogynist foundations of the practices, pimps perceived that the power and status associated with their pimp mobiles aided their quest to acquire the service of prostitutes. They commonly purchased luxury cars, most prominently Cadillacs, and transformed them into elaborately dressed machines. These cars featured such modifications as custom grills, "goddess" hood ornaments, whitewall tires, spoked chrome wheels, and high-end stereo systems.

More so than music, pimps and pimp mobiles were common themes within Blaxploitation, the genre of African American–themed films that depicted the lives of Black outlaw heroes. Pimp culture was a common theme as it was central to the plots of popular films such as *Superfly*, *The Mack*, and *Willie Dynamite*. Reflecting reality, these characters' cars were presented as being important parts of their identities and their effectiveness as pimps. For example, in *Superfly* (1972), the character Priest drove an unforgettable 1971 Cadillac Eldorado customized with a chrome grill, "goddess" hood ornament, and headlight covers. *Willie Dynamite* (1974) features a classic scene in which Pimp Willie drives up in his customized purple Cadillac and parks in front of his residence. He is greeted by neighborhood kids who marvel at the sight of his car. When one of the kids claims that he's going to get a Cadillac for himself, Willie responds, "Well, you better start stealing your mama's milk money."

Black pimps were cultural anti-heroes among many Black working-class male youths searching for power and meaning. "Having seen *Super Fly* that summer at the Loew's Victoria of 125th Street, a decaying bijou a few doors down from the Apollo Theater, I wanted to be as in vogue as the peacock pimps I passed on the block," journalist Michael Gonzales critically reminisces (2007, 101). He later notes that pimps "with their sleek Cadillacs painted in screaming colors and sporting flashy hubcaps, were a sight to see" (102). The pimp mobile is at the foundations of the modified car cultures that emerged in areas such as Houston, Memphis, Miami, and Atlanta in the mid-1980s. This next generation of the Black male youths appropriated the pimp mobile to reflect the particulars of their social world. "The first slabs were all pimp cars, we just modernized it as time went on, venturing out in different ways and with different cars, but it all started from pimp culture," notes Big Love (interview with the author, 2021).

Slabs did not emerge in a vacuum, however, as car customization was already a common practice in the Houston streets. "Originally it was low riders, then it was the Cherokee lines. You had the green Cherokee line and the red Cherokee line. These were Jeep Cherokee trucks," says China Boy. The rise of crack combined with the emergence of swangas to produce slab culture, which quickly transformed the cultural politics of the Houston streets and created long-lasting urban tradition.

China Boy was able to easily rattle off early Southside slab riders and their contribution to the culture as we sat at Starbucks in Houston's fancy "new" Midtown neighborhood some thirty years later:

> There was this one guy that really got it started and that was Toast. It was Toast and then this guy named Corey Blount. And that was Toast. That was him and this guy named Corey Blount. They used to have slant

backs. Corey Blount, you'll never seen him again in life. Like, I'm pretty sure you know who he is. You'll never see him again in life. They used to call Corey Blount the slab king. He was the slab King. I knew Corey. You know, I knew Toast. I knew them personally. Toast, Corey Blount, Keith Babins, Rafael Branch—I knew all those people personally because I hung around. I hung around in that area through my cousin Trent. I knew Smitty, Andre Pfeiffer, and Kenneth Bell. See Kenneth Bell was the first one with a "Boss Hogg" Cadillac. Yeah, he was great. He was the first one with the ball Sol Cadillac. His was a smoke gray with discs and vogues on it. He had four twelves in his car. And his four twelves sounded like he had eight fifteens in it. See, my friend Fish, he couldn't pull up on the side of him. (Interview with the author, 2013).

The above named are part of the Black Houston's Street mythology. Each of them has his own unique story, but their slabs helped solidify their cultural power both then and now. In many ways, slab culture was the perfect representation of the autonomous culture of the Southside streets. The cars were idiosyncratic indexes of the social and economic relationship between street actors, a relationship undergirded by the struggle for power. "You're a big-time drug dealer? You sell drugs? You got to get your Cadillac. You got to get some gold. You got to get you a woman on the side, and you got to get you some music. You've got to get those things because you got the money to do it," China Boy says about the origins of slab. P Izm agrees: "I saw guys like Toast, Q-Dog and you know, a few other guys over there in SA riding slab. So ever since then, I was just hooked. I was like, well, you know, once I get me a little money that's the first thing I'm gonna do. I didn't want to get a house first or none of that. You know what I mean? I wanted a slab so and that's what I did" (interview with the author, 2013).

The potential for social mobility inherent to riding slab was limited to the streets. Within mainstream culture, their function as a status marker, as well as their aesthetic beauty, was not acknowledged. For those of the streets, however, acquiring a slab represented the matriculation into a higher order. They were men above the rest, individuals to be respected, admired, and in some cases, feared. As E.S.G. notes, "We all looked up to the D-Boys [drug dealers] because they had the freshest slabs."

Almost forty years later, slab continues to reflect a unique, intercultural marker of social and economic status within the Houston streets (Wilkins

2016). In mainstream life, cars like Maseratis, Bentleys, and Mercedes Benzes are markers of success, making them valuable forms of social capital. In the Houston streets, such cars do not have the same level of social cache when compared to slabs. "You got females that will pass up that Benz, to go get in that slab," says Big Be. "You can pull them Bentleys, you can pull them Maseratis, but when that drop come through ... over with." Some of the slabs' value is rooted in the perceived vulnerability that comes with ownership. "Any square can get in a Bentley or a Benz. A square can't drive in a drop. 'Cause somebody'd take it," says Dunta (interview with the author, 2013). Slabs, in this sense, hold a significant amount of cultural capital that is informed by wealth and a certain level of street knowledge.

Slabs also exist outside of street culture, becoming a Black working-class practice that reflects several layers of meaning (Wilkins 2016). Sometimes lost in discussion of the street and power is the fact that, at its core, slab is a creative expression of the self. "You fix your car up to match your personality," P Izm the Mack made plain. Big Love elaborates on that notion: "It's something that you create. It's just the whole creative process." Keeping within the larger Black car-culture continuum, slab also functions as a symbolic form of uplift, a symbol of class aspirations. "A slab shows that as a hustler or working man, I have arrived and here is my crown." Over forty years in, slab is also a tradition. Young men and an increasing number of women are learning the tradition from middle-aged elders. "It's a rite of passage," Big Be tells me (interview with the author, 2013).

Building community and "reppin' the 'hood" is a core value within slab culture. I witnessed this firsthand during the Slab Holiday event in Galveston, Texas, on May 19, 2012. Slab Holiday was one of the many slab-related events that took place in and around Houston that year. From what I was told, however, it was certainly one of the largest. There were hundreds of slabs on the beach that day, and most of them presented some direct connection to Houston neighborhoods. The aforementioned trunk displays were probably the most intelligible expression of place, for an outsider like myself at least. Many of these trunk displays made note of the owners' neighborhood of origin, social groups from those neighborhoods, memorials to fallen associates, and neighborhood values.

This green Slab in Figure 6 expresses place along several lines. The glass display situated inside the trunk contains the phrases "Trinity Garden Still

Figure 6. Green slab at Slab Holiday in Galveston, Texas, on May 19, 2012. Photo by author.

Stunt'n" and "Weaver Boyz." Trinity Gardens is a neighborhood on the North-side of Houston, close to Fifth Ward, and Weaver Road is a notable street within it. The "Weaver Boyz" is likely a reference to an informal social group that emerged from that street. "Stunt'n," as it is used in the display, means to present material possessions as a marker of success or achievement. So, in short, when read in conjunction with the neon sign on the inner hood of the trunk, the phrase "Trinity Garden Still Stunt'n" suggests that the owner identifies with his neighborhood and that his marker of success (the slab) is the neighborhood's as well.

The earliest arriving cars at Slab Holiday appeared to be presented in iso-lation. They made solo, unattached entrances and they parked in arbitrary positions, seemingly unrelated to the other cars in their proximity. About an hour or so into the event, I noticed a change. There appeared to be some sort of organization to the cars entering the beach. Groups of cars (four to seven) of the same color appeared to be entering together, in a very slow manner, with each sound system at full blast. Upon entering the beach, they parked side by side in a fashion that allowed them to show group strength but retain individual identity. Even some of the previously stationed cars began lining

Figure 7. Green line at Slab Holiday in Galveston, Texas, on May 19, 2012. Photo by author.

up with these groups. As I later learned, these were slab lines, a fundamental part of the culture.

Lines, in slab culture, are informal car clubs. They are groups of various sizes that share paint color and typically originate from the same neighborhood or area. China Boy gave me a brief survey of the various lines of the moment: "Slab lines are just car clubs. The only difference is you got Northside blue, Southside red, Southwest red, Southeast teal or whatever you got. You got different lines. You have Northside blue and then they got a Northside orange. They got a burnt orange line. ... Let's say you get a box of crayons and set it right here. They got a line for every couple of crayons in the box."

During informal events like block parties and slab meetups, a single slab line will proceed down the street, with member cars lined up one after another, and then attempt to park themselves in a single area. During formal events like car shows, slab lines proceed into an event in a straight line. They position themselves as a unit. They then exit an event in the same fashion. While swangin', a type of processional play whereby the cars weave from lane to lane in a dawdling manner, slab lines move together in a display of community unity.

I also want to point out a less conspicuous example of how slab reflects community. I initially struggled to connect with the slab community. I would see the cars everywhere in the field and talked to several slab riders about my work, but I consistently failed to schedule any formal conversations. It was clear that I was a cultural outsider and just did not have the vulnerable community's trust. On a whim, I reached out to OG Scott about this, and he told me to drop by his house a couple of nights later. When I got to Scott's home in Cleveland that night, I quickly realized that a whole world had been opened to me. There were about ten slabs of various makes, models, and colors. The slab riders parked and exited their vehicles leaving the doors open so I could explore on my own. A few even swang through the street. All of them greeted Scott with much reverence. Being a longtime Cloverland resident and a noted street figure turned servant, Scott held much respect and power. He used his cultural power.

I want to conclude this section with the words of my friend Big Love, who offers a touching testament to the meaning and purpose of slab:

> When we were kids, there's a game we played called Bingo. Whenever a nice car came by, you would point at it and go "Bingo!" And when you said bingo, that means that car was yours. So, when the next nice car came down the street, your friend might beat you to it and say bingo. It was just a competition to symbolically own the baddest cars around. So, the slabs are kind of like our bingo in reality. It's like, we're no longer looking at somebody else's car and going bingo and wishing one day it was ours. We now own them. Our inspiration came from poverty. It's hope. It's hope and inspiration that one day, I'm going to be able to own a vehicle that clean. So, when you're old enough to get the money to do the thing that you want to do, then you want to own a slab. Your hopes and your aspirations are now materialized. Now it's in front of you, you're the owner. There's no better feeling than having a hope and a dream and an accomplishment. So, a slab is an accomplishment of thoughts that we conceived way back when we were children.

SLABS AND HOUSTON HIP HOP

In the mid-1990s, the slab scene and the local hip hop scene became inextricably tied, fused together by artists who were as deep in the streets as they were in the rap game. As I noted in an earlier chapter, Screwed Up Click members frequently mentioned slabs in their freestyles, helping to popularize the practice in the city. "The Southside were my fans and I got them listening to what I'm saying," Lil Randy told me. "Just like the Screwtapes went to a massive, red cars went to a massive, and people screaming the Southside went to a massive" (interview with the author, 2012).

Slabs became even more popular once S.U.C.-related artists began releasing commercial music. Local labels like Jam Down, Wreckshop, and Chevis Entertainment began to sign local artists who explicitly embraced the burgeoning screw culture. One such artist was E.S.G. Born Cedric Hill in Bogalusa, Louisiana, E.S.G. moved to the Southside of Houston as a teenager. At the time, according to E.S.G., "The southside was playa" (interview with the author, March 2012). So E.S.G. sought to record a song that "included everything pertaining to the culture and place we were living in." That song became 1994's "Swangin' N Bangin'," a documentation of and dedication to the Southside slab scene.

Produced by Sean "Solo" Jemison, "Swangin' n Bangin'" offers a vivid description of the slab scene. The title and chorus, "swangin' n bangin'," refers to the practices of "swangin'," which involves driving at extremely low speeds while weaving from lane to lane, and "bangin'," playing your stereo at high volumes to sonically announce your presence. Throughout the song, E.S.G. details core elements of slab aesthetics including 84s, vogue tires, bubble headlights, fifth wheels, grills, and candy paint. The music video, released as a remixed version in 1995, reconstructs a typical slab gathering: lots of cars, lots of women, and much music. "Swangin' N Bangin'" was originally released in screwed and regular form on E.S.G.'s 1994 album *Ocean of Funk* on local Perrion Records. Regionally distributed through local Southwest Wholesale, *Ocean of Funk* went on to sell 100,000 copies in Houston and throughout the South. In 1995, the album was reconstructed and rereleased as *Sailin' the South* with national distribution through Priority Records. "Swangin' N Bangin'" was able to gain significant radio play, and *Sailing the South* doubled the sales of *Ocean of Funk*. The immense popularity of "Swangin' N Bangin'" and later slab anthems like Big Mello's "Wegonefunkwichamind" and Fat Pat's "Tops Drop" helped cement slab as a core part of Houston hip hop identity both in and out of town.

As Big Love notes: "The SUC and those guys are the originators of rapping in context about these cars. Before them, there was nobody else you know talking about the elbows and swaying, candy paint and the interior. So those guys were folklorists, the storytellers, and originators of putting these concepts and these vehicles in the music" (interview with the author, 2021). The music helped grow the culture, moving it away from the streets and opening participation to folks from all walks of life.

SLABS, HIP HOP, and COMMUNITY CONFLICT

Slab, at its core, is about community building and celebration. In the mid-1990s, however, the cars were the source of an intense, and often violent, conflict between the Southside and the Northside. Tensions between the two sides of town go back several generations, but they rarely went beyond petty rivalry, the kind that would appear during sports competitions. These relatively benign tensions turned to full-out war when, as E.S.G. tells me, several Southside red slabs were stolen and found stripped of their various components in Northside neighborhoods such as Rosewood. "There was a lot of SLABs on the Southside that were being stole by cats from the Northside. I cannot think of the neighborhood in particular, but yeah that's what it was. ... That's when the tension became really big. 'Cause a car would get stolen on the Southside and it would get found stripped on the Northside" (E.S.G., interview with the author, March 2012). P Izm the Mack, a native of the Southside's South Acres neighborhood who was very active in the streets during this period, supports E.S.G.'s general overview with a personal account of his involvement in the Northside/Southside conflict. "I had my first slab six or seven years before some Northside cats stole it," he told me. "It was found stripped somewhere in the Northside. In Fifth Ward I think" (interview with the author, December 2013).

P Izm the Mack relates another anecdote that suggests that economics was not the sole source of the Northside-on-Southside violence:

> I got into a shoot-out on the freeway once. In a slab. I was ridin' slab and I had hats in the back that said South Acres. You know, I was representin' my 'hood. These Northside dudes rode on the side of me and were tryin' to run into my car. This was on [highway] 59. I had to start bustin' on

'em. It was that bad man. If they couldn't steal your slab, they didn't want you to have it. They were going to try to destroy it. (Interview with the author, December 2013)

The individuals P Izm describes as Northsiders were not attempting to steal his car. That would be a futile effort on such a busy highway. They simply did not want him to have it. He seems to suggest that this attempted vandalism was informed by jealousy. It is also likely that being credited with destroying a Southsider's slab, especially in such a violent way, could increase their respect in the Northside streets.

The Screwed Up Click was entrenched in the Southside streets and, therefore, impacted severely by the rash of slab thefts. Members Fat Pat, Lil Keke, Lil Randy, and Stick 1 were all very respected within the slab scene. Corey Blount, a non-rapping member of the Screwed Up Click, was considered the "Slab King" because he allegedly owned nearly a dozen fully customized vehicles. Considering the importance of slab within their group as well as on the Southside streets, members of the Screwed Up Click began addressing the car thefts on screwtapes. According to Lil Randy, "The Northside been stealing cars from the Southside for as long as I can remember. It's just that one day someone got fed up with it and said it on a Screwtape" (interview with the author, April 2012). The "someone" Lil Randy refers to is Fat Pat, who first publicly commented on the slab-fueled Northside/Southside conflict during a freestyle on DJ Screw's *Wineberry Over Gold* (1995):

> Them Northside niggas, they comin' over here flippin'
> Tryin' to run our set, but nigga you can bet
> It's time to grab the gats and gon' make a nigga wet
> It's like the pistol, grab the fuckin' pump

In this selection, Fat Pat lyrically represents, defends, and mobilizes his Southside 'hood. He explicitly indicts the Northside for the rampant carjacking within the Southside slab community. He urges his Southside audience, including those not involved in the slab scene, to view these carjackings as a mark of disrespect and then challenges them to defend their 'hood's honor through violence. Fat Pat's freestyle is a call to arms. He verbally declares that within the Southside streets, such disrespect will be met with force.

Fat Pat's freestyle rap in *Wineberry Over Gold* was an initial thrust in what was to become a common practice of the Screwed Up Click dissing the

Northside on screwtapes. Most of these disses were rather benign, rooted in the ritual insult gaming practice that is part of African American oral tradition and hip hop culture. Other performances, however, were much more explicit, surpassing the level of violence presented in Fat Pat's freestyle. For example, in the following freestyle from DJ Screw's *Leanin' On a Switch*, Lil Keke warns the Northside against returning to the Southside to steal additional cars:

> Northside, if you hear me, you ain't sippin' on Robotussin
> You ain't playa, never parlayin'
> Southside done found out where you bustas stayin'
> In that Rosewood, disrespectin' 'hoods

In the above selection, Lil Keke states that he and his fellow Southsiders are ready and willing to violently defend their territory. In the following freestyle, S.U.C. member Big Pokey takes an offensive approach:

> Comin' through they 'hood and I'm sittin' sideways
> Gotta make my mail, ounces gon' swell
> I'm come through and shoot up the Tidwell
> Shoot up Cavalcade, 'cause I done got paid

Here, Big Pokey raps about using an assault rifle (AK-47) to unleash a violent attack on Tidwell and Cavalcade streets, two important areas in the Northside's street space. Such verbal threats aimed at the Northside were commonplace on screwtapes in the mid-1990s. Through expressions of imagined violence, Lil Keke, Big Pokey, Fat Pat, and other members of the Screwed Up Click proudly represented and symbolically safeguarded their Southside 'hood.

The Screwed Up Click's verbal assault toward the Northside went unanswered until a group of Northside artists—calling themselves Swishahouse—began to fight back through their own slowed-down mixtapes. Northside DJs Michael "5000" Watts and OG Ron C started Swishahouse in 1997. Reflecting a grounding in the streets, the name Swishahouse is derived from the Northside marijuana distribution houses that many called swisha houses. In the late 1990s, Michael Watts and OG Ron C began producing screwed mixtapes in the vein of DJ Screw. These mixtapes featured slowed versions of hit songs along with freestyles from their roster of Northside rap artists that then included Slim Thug, J-Dawg, Lil Mario, and Archie Lee among others.

During a segment on the Northside/Southside beef from the popular *Beef* documentary series, Michael Watts notes that Swishahouse mixtapes were made for Northside audiences who enjoyed the screwed sounds, but detested the verbal assaults aimed their way: "A lot of people on the Northside did listen to Screwtapes, but there were a couple of them where they were plexing against the Northside. Of course, if somebody's gonna be doggin' you, you're not gonna listen to that shit" (QDIII 2007).

Swishahouse artists responded to the Screwed Up Click's insults and threats by cultivating a distinctly Northside street identity. Whereas the Screwed Up Click rapped about bald-fade haircuts, Swishahouse artists rapped about braids and afros, two hairstyles popular among Northside young adults. Swishahouse rappers vociferously celebrated Northside neighborhoods like Acres Homes, Greenspoint, and Rosewood. While red slabs marked Southside identity, Swishahouse made blue slabs a marker of the Northside streets.

The hostility between the Screwed Up Click and Swishahouse intensified after DJ Screw died of a codeine overdose on November 16, 2000. Swishahouse's Michael Watts became the public face of screw music and, according to journalist Roni Sarig, Michael Watts and OG Ron C "were arguably more famous nationally for making screw music than Screw was" (Sarig 2007, 325). As Paul Wall recalls, "Southside against Northside was more like ... it was like straight-up gang violence. Bloods versus Crips" (QDIII 2007). There were essentially two sectors of hip hop production in Houston, one in the North and one in the South. Rarely did the two collaborate.

This territorial conflict lasted into the new millennium, and the peace process involved interventions from multiple sectors. In 2000 a California company, Texan Wire Wheels, began reproducing and mass-manufacturing both the 83 and 84 swangas, which reduced their base retail price from $10,000 to around $3,000 for a set of four. This decrease in price and exclusiveness made them less attractive to carjackers. Also in 2000, Houston-area HBCU Prairie View A & M University attempted to intervene with the Stop the Set Trippin', a conference that featured Northside and Southside rappers peacefully discussing their differences in front of a crowd of students. Big Love represented the Northside at the event and felt that it was an important step in calming tensions. "My Northside people got to see that all that flexing is over and we're moving on to something new," he says. In addition, Northside and Southside rappers began to collaborate with hopes that such partnerships would help unite the streets. In 2001, E.S.G. and Slim Thug released *Boss Hogg Outlawz*, an album that was very popular on both sides of town. City unity, according to E.S.G., was the inspiration behind the album: "We were just trying to bring the city back together. It was like, damn, niggas were always into some carjacking or something. So niggas was like, fuck it, let's find somebody from the North and do a collabo album of something" (interview with the author, March 2012).

Relatedly, rap artists from both camps had begun moving away from producing mixtapes, which consisted of freestyles over other previously recorded material, to producing commercial releases of original music. They released albums through local independent labels such as Jam Down, Wreckshop, and Suckafree as well as Swishahouse that were distributed through regional companies such as Southwest Wholesale or national distributors like Universal and Priority. In short, artists like Slim Thug, Lil Keke, E.S.G., and Paul Wall became fully professional rap artists with national fanbases. As such, they had little interest in local territorial conflicts.

"STILL TIPPIN'" and THE Mainstreaming OF HOUSTON'S HIP HOP HERITAGE

Through the first few years of the 2000s, the Houston hip hop scene had a fickle relationship with the mainstream hip-hop landscape. Intermittently, records would bubble up out of the city, make a mark in the South, and then get respectable radio spins around the country. The Geto Boys' *Mind Playin' Tricks* (1991) was the first of such records. Written by members Scarface and Willie D, the song is a haunting yet funky exposition on the precarious nature of street life and the resulting psychological effects of engagement in it. The song reached #1 on Billboard's Hot Rap Singles chart and #23 on the Hot 100. The equally haunting video received regular play on hip hop video vehicles *Yo! MTV Raps* and *Rap City*. This helped cement Rap-A-Lot Records as an important hip hop label both locally and nationally.

Outside of Rap-A-Lot, mainstream was rarified air for local artists. In 1998, a collaboration between Screwed Up Click members Fat Pat, Hawk, and Yungstar along with Lil Will and Big T called "Wanna Be a Baller" almost cracked the Top 40 on the Billboard charts, and the corresponding video received regular play on BET and MTV. Other songs such as DJ DMD's "25

Lighters" and Big Moe's "Purple Stuff" received lukewarm mainstream attention at best.

The reasons behind Houston hip hop's lack of mainstream presence are twofold. First, Houston has long employed an independent ethos. Artists have been able to find immense success by selling records locally and regionally. As a result, they felt little need to engage New York and Los Angeles, the two centers of the mainstream hip hop market. Second, the mainstream hip hop landscape had long been resistant to the sounds coming from the South.

The Houston hip hop scene managed to break through these cultural limitations and became the center of the hip hop landscape between 2005 and 2007. Music by artists such as Paul Wall, Chamillionaire, and Lil Flip dominated the airwaves, charts, and television. Artists appeared in numerous magazine articles, including a legendary April 2006 cover article in *The Source*, appropriately titled "Don't Mess with Texas." Like Compton in 1989, the Houston hip hop scene was in vogue. And it all started with a simple remix called "Still Tippin'" by Mike Jones, Paul Wall, and Slim Thug.

The evolution of "Still Tippin'" parallels the evolution of Swishahouse as a record label. After numerous successful mixtapes, Swishahouse formed as a record label in 1999 and included most of their original Northside rhymers on their roster. The new label's very first release was a compilation called *The Day Hell Broke Loose* (1999). In 2003, through a partnership with Rap A Lot Records, the label released *The Day After Hell Broke Loose*, which contained a funky yet relatively mediocre song called "Still Tippin'" performed by Slim Thug, Chamillionaire, and new affiliate Mike Jones. Later in 2003, Swishahouse signed a national distribution deal with the Southern hip hop–friendly Asylum Records, a recently reactivated division of Warner Brothers Records. To celebrate their new deal, which in some ways was a rebirth, Swishahouse released another sequel to *The Day Hell Broke Loose*, appropriately called *The Day Hell Broke Loose 2*. Like the original, the album featured Swishahouse's stable of Northside emcees, but reflecting squashed beefs, the album also featured appearances by Screwed Up Click members Lil Keke and Lil Flip. *The Day Hell Broke Loose 2* featured a remixed version of "Still Tippin'," this time featuring Chamillionaire's former rhyme partner Paul Wall. Despite this original placement, the song began to garner major buzz when it was released in late 2004 as the first single from Mike Jones's debut album *Who Is Mike Jones?* (2005).

The success of "Still Tippin'" did not occur by happenstance, nor was it purely due to musical appeal. Rather, a perfect storm of hip hop and pop-cultural shifts laid the groundwork for Houston's mid-decade rise into the mainstream. First was the ascendancy of Southern hip hop as a major commercial force in the late 1990s. Long commercially and critically subjugated, Southern hip hop scenes began to attain greater cultural relevance beginning with New Orleans in 1998. Both No Limit Records and Cash Money Records found national success by mixing the local bounce music sound with gangsta-based lyrics. New Orleans–based artists such as No Limit's Master P and Mystikal as well as Cash Money's Juvenile, B.G., and Lil Wayne all found platinum success between 1998 and 2000s. There's some debate as to which regional centers initiated the rise of southern hip hop. I argue that the commercial dominance of two New Orleans–based labels, No Limit and Cash Money, opened the door for the rest of the South.

Also notable was the appearance of MTV's *Pimp My Ride* in 2004, around the same time "Still Tippin'" was released as a commercial single. The show offered Middle America a look, albeit extreme, into the world of urban car modification.

On "Still Tippin'," slab acts as a symbolic packaging through which Slim Thug, Paul Wall, Mike Jones, and producer Salih Williams synthesize the various elements of local identity into a coherent and tangible commercial product. The title and hook, which frames the song, was taken from an old Slim Thug freestyle and slowed by DJ Michael Watts. "Still Tippin of fo fos, wrapped in fo vogues" is a direct reference to slab aesthetics: four 84s which are wrapped in four vogue tires. The slab references do not end there. In the song's second verse, Mike Jones raps about "lane switching with the paint dripping" and in an even more direct fashion "slab shinin' with the grille and woman." Salih Williams's syrupy infectious beat employs a slowed sample of the *William Tell Overture* to sonically represent the sluggishly psychedelic feeling that is said to occur when listening to screw and/or consuming lean. Lean is explicitly referenced during Slim Thug (barre sippin) and Mike Jones's (syrup sippin) verses. But while present, the screw and lean are couched within references to slab. As music journalist Sasha Frere-Jones writes, "Still Tippin' is an elegant primer on Houston hip-hop" (2005). "Still Tippin'" ultimately is a compiled and curated manifestation of Houston hip hop identity dressed in slab culture.

The video for "Still Tippin'" helped reinforce the exoticness of the song. Directed by Houston-based Dr. Teeth, the music video harkens back to E.S.G.'s "Swangin' N Bangin." The three MCs along with DJ Michael Watts are joined by several hundred spectators in a setting that mimics a typical H-Town slab gathering. Carefully placed slabs provide the backdrop for the rappers' performances. In addition, footage of a slab processional is spliced in throughout the video.

"Still Tippin'" took the hip hop world by storm. The song reached #26 on Billboard's "Hot Hip Hop & R&B" chart and peaked at #26 on its "Hot 100" pop chart. The video received constant rotation on MTV and BET. For the first time in years, national media began paying attention to hip hop in Houston. Notable hip hop–centered publications like *The Source* and *Vibe Magazine* ran several articles that featured Slim Thug, Paul Wall, and Mike Jones throughout 2005. Benjamin Meadows-Ingram wrote a particularly in-depth feature on the trio for *Vibe* that contended that "Still Tippin'" "finally lead Houston's original sluggish sound to the promised land of national exposure" (Meadows-Ingram 2005). Kaleefa Sanneh wrote a notable piece for the *New York Times* called "The Strangest Sound in Hip Hop Goes National," which used "Still Tippin'" to introduce and survey the larger Houston scene. Similarly, Sasha Frere-Jones's *New Yorker* piece "A Place in the Sun" compares the way "Still Tippin'" brought Houston's hip hop identity to national prominence to the way Nirvana did the same for Seattle.

In the immediate wake of the success of "Still Tippin'," slab became a pivot point that allowed Houston-based artists to negotiate their place within mainstream hip hop. Mike Jones's first album *Who Is Mike Jones?* debuted at #3 on the pop chart on the strength of "Still Tippin'" along with his second single "Back Then," which also features several references to slab culture. Former Swishahouse affiliate Chamillionaire used slab culture to protest police harassment on "Ridin," which became a number 1 single and Grammy award–winning song. Paul Wall, however, could have been considered the pop culture slab king. His debut album *The People's Champ* rose to the top of the pop charts on the strength of its lead single "Sittin Sidewayz." The song, which featured Screwed Up Click member Big Pokey, followed the model that "Still Tippin'" established. Thematically it was rooted in slab culture, as the phrase "sittin sideways" refers to the way slab riders position their bodies as they are driving. Also like "Still Tippin'," the hook employed a sample of an old freestyle; this time it was Big Pokey's performance on the iconic DJ Screw *June 27* mixtape. The song and video were immensely popular and helped Paul Wall's *The People's Champ* debut at #1 on Billboard's Hot 200 in the fall of 2005. Ironically, *The People's Champ* knocked Kanye West's *Late Registration*, which included Paul Wall dropping a slab-fueled verse on "Drive Slow," off the top of the pop chart. For Houston artists, slab proved to be the perfect mix of the exotic and the familiar. It created a workable space for them within popular culture and they actively used it to release several platinum and multi-platinum albums over a two-year span.

Houston's reign in the mainstream was short-lived as exoticism proved to be an unsustainable model. By 2008, Houston's presence within the national hip hop landscape was virtually untraceable. It is a bit difficult to pinpoint the reasons Houston artists could not continue their mainstream mobility. Several of the artists that I talked to felt that the music released during the city's mainstream reign did not offer enough variety and national audiences became bored. "The movement was in the wrong hands and it lacked originality," Lil Randy told me with hesitation. Journalist Roni Sarig agrees: "As 2005's hype marked Houston as the next hot music mecca, it became increasingly clear that—despite some impressive chart showings—if all Houston had to offer was candy paint, sipping syrup, and gold grills, the focus would turn elsewhere" (2007, 336). Others, like EDF, felt that it is just hard for cities outside of New York, Los Angeles, and Atlanta to have consistent national impact. "Those other cities have people in place to help you make power moves," he says. "It's all political at the end of the day."

Houston hip hop has a fiercely independent spirit, and Houston-based artists have turned inward—focusing their efforts on retaining cultural identity and cultivating local audiences. Slab naturally has become a vehicle through which these efforts are carried out. "The swangas are a part of our identity in Houston," says Dunta. "Wherever we go, we bring the swings up so everyone knows we're from Houston" (interview with the author, 2012). The Bloc Boyz Click's "Officially Ridin' Swings," Yella Fella's "Slab Is Beautiful" and the Botany Boyz' "Ridin Slab" are among the many songs about slab culture that have been released over the last ten years. Paul Wall and Lil Keke dedicated a whole album to slab, appropriately titled *Slab Talk*. Even Houston-bred international superstars Megan Thee Stallion, Travis Scott, and Beyonce have featured slab in their recordings, photoshoots, and music videos.

E.S.G.'s 2018 song and video "Southside Still Holdin'" highlights the impact of slab on Houston hip hop culture and could be considered a form of heritage work. As in "Swangin' N Bangin'," he makes lyrical references to slab, screw, and lean while shouting out the various Black neighborhoods around the city. This time, however, E.S.G. makes it a point to mention old-school slab riders like the Bubba Twins, Toast, and Corey Blount, who was released from federal prison in 2020 after serving time for a nonviolent drug offense. E.S.G.'s tribute works to ensure that their contributions remain a part of cultural memory even as the culture grows and changes. The song's remix places older legends, including Bun B, Lil O, Lil Flip, and Slim Thug, alongside younger artists like Trilly Poke and Dat Boi T (aka The Screwed Up Essay). This intergenerational collaboration is a symbolic form of cultural sustenance.

Slab began as a small group street practice and quickly became part of Houston's local hip hop identity both within the city and around the country. Now, local artists and private citizens are actively working to define slab as a civic heritage, hoping to ensure its cultural vitality in proceeding generations.

4

GOTTA COME DOWN, GOTTA REP THE HOOD

Been reppin' this shit since from the start
Married to the game, can't tear us apart
Grew up in the H, I love the H
That's why it's tatted right by my heart.
—Dunta of the Bloc Boyz Click,
"Purple Swag (S.U.C. Houston Edition)"

"We got our own thang, own style, and even our own drugs," says rapper Dunta regarding Houston's hip hop scene. "We ain't like nobody else" (interview with the author, April 2012). This Houston hip hop bravado is reflected in the music that he makes as part of the Bloc Boyz Click. Consisting of members Adrian, Al, Feva, Gospa Man, and Big Be, the Bloc Boyz are a quintessential Houston rap group. Their sound and style are firmly rooted in the local screw tradition. Over beats laid by producer Lil Kano, the Bloc Boyz bear lyrical witness to the dynamics of street life in Houston, Texas.

Although their headquarters are in Southside's Cloverland neighborhood, group members hail from all over Houston. Members Big Be, Dunta, and Feva along with Cloverland Records label owner OG Scott are from Cloverland. Adrian is from "TABB City," a colloquial name given to four Southside streets that form a square near Houston's Hobby Airport. Big Be insisted to me that, besides talent, it is their multiplaced constitution that gives the group its power: "That's the hook of the group. 'Cause the group name is the Bloc Boyz, so what we tried to do is incorporate all blocks of the city. Ya know, it really just came together like that. It's a blessing. We were able to put one group together and represent the whole city" (interview with the author, March 2012). Therefore, embodied in the Bloc Boyz name is a cross section of the Houston "streets." This is their "hook" or one of the ways they garner attention within the scene. By including multiple neighborhoods and areas in their group, they seek to build a diverse fan base.

The Bloc Boyz Click are among the many street-based local artists that fervently adhere to the screw heritage. Sonically, their production styles are heavily influenced by screw music: mid-tempo, melodic, and atmospheric. It is also common for them to remix their songs using the screwed & chopped technique. Their lyrics are grounded in the social dynamics of the local streets and prominently feature depictions of violence and drug dealing. In addition, slabs and syrup are prevalent themes. Reflecting the screw tradition, "reppin your 'hood" remains a key practice for street artists. These artists actively and explicitly mention the various spaces and places that they hold dear including apartment buildings, streets, neighborhoods, and the entire city of Houston. They present these areas as core parts of their personal identity. In this chapter, I critically analyze the myriad ways Houston's street artists represent these spaces and places through recordings, live performance, and interpersonal interactions.

MY SIDE OF TOWN

Rapper Rob Gullatte and I are similar people on paper. The intersections are numerous. We both are brown-skinned Black men who were born and raised in Houston, Texas. We both lived transient lives, moving around from Black neighborhood to Black neighborhood until we settled on the Southwest side of town. He grew up in Alief while I, as previously mentioned, came of age in Hiram Clarke. And hip hop played a central role in both of our social lives and continues to form a central part of our adult careers.

The similarities are limited, however. I lived a rather square existence. I was raised in a lower-middle-class household with two educated parents. Given this structure and security, I was able to focus on school, played on my high school tennis team, and looked toward college. Rob's youth was quite different. Raised by a single mother struggling to provide, he spent much of his youth moving from home to home in various areas throughout the Southside of Houston. "We were kind of nomads," he tells me. "We moved neighborhood to neighborhood." Like many other youths, economic and domestic instability pushed him into street life at a very early age. At 11 and

12, he was selling single marijuana joints to folks in his neighborhood. He worked under an older guy who would give him a hundred sweets to sell at three for $10. But in no time he graduated to selling crack. "I was never . . . like a big-time drug dealer, you know what I'm sayin'," he tells me. "I did it because I wanted money. My mama was hurtin'. And I was too young to work" (interview with the author, July 2018).

For Gullatte, a sense of normalcy was fleeting. His youth was defined by a type of yin and yang not uncommon for many young Black men living in Alief, better known as the SWATS by local residents. He went to school, first going to the demographically diverse Elsik in Alief and then later transferring to newly opened Westside High School. He was in church every Sunday. He also took basketball pretty seriously. "I got pretty good at it. I'm not saying I would've made the NBA or anything, but." However, on any given night, you would find him in the streets selling crack and powder cocaine, trying to scrape up a living for himself and his family.

Living the street life entails an incessant and inescapable engagement with death. Gullatte had to hold his own during turf wars, robberies, and jealousies that put his life in constant danger. "It was a lot of fights, then when you start going to the club and you start seeing niggas from other areas and y'all start gettin' into it. It was just a lot of drama, man." He often had to use violence to safeguard his life. "I ain't even like kill nobody or nothing like that, but I done bust my gun enough to know that I would've killed somebody if it came into play" he somberly tells me (Gullatte, interview with the author, July 2018). While he was able to survive the streets, many of his friends and associates were not. One such friend was Colton Opuni, one of Gullatte's best friends who happens to have attended Sidney Lanier Middle School with me. In May of 2003, Colton was found dead in the trunk of his own car after being missing for three days. Colton and Rob were supposed to hang out the night he disappeared. The loss hit him hard. "I had lost people before that, and some of them were close friends. But, Colton was like my brother, that wasn't just a nigga I was in the streets with," he says. "To this day, I still feel a certain way about that because my dude just didn't get an opportunity to grow up out of what he was becoming" (Gullatte, interview with the author, 2018).

For Gullatte, the poverty, the hustling, the cultural diversity, the relationships built, and the friends lost in Alief are what helped make him a man.

"Outside of crime and all that, it's still a great place to grow up. There are some good people there," he stresses to me (interview with the author, July 2018). Therefore he makes it a point to center the neighborhood in his life and in his music. "It's very important that people know that I'm from Alief and that I represent it because that is what my personality is, mayne" he tells me. "I'm diverse and all that. But, I'll still get on your ass. Like, never forget that. I'll still get on your ass. That's the spirit of Alief." This is also true in his music. Through several independent releases, Gullatte has consistently celebrated SWATS and the larger Southwest Houston community. This most often takes place in the form of casual references to the neighborhood, but "My Side of Town," from his 2014 album *Abortion: The Project*, is a raw and unadulterated celebration of his 'hood. Produced by Fred the Producer, "My Side of Town" paints a complex portrait of the area:

> Southwest of the Astrodome
> Outside the loop where we invade your home
> Where the Esses is and the Asians roam
> Where the licks is plenty and the paper long

In four bars, Gullatte synthesizes the two most popular and polarizing conceptions of Southwest Houston. He references the sizeable Mexican American and Asian American communities in the Southwest who, along with residents from the African diaspora, make up the Southwest Houston's most diverse area. At the same time, he portrays the West as a place where home invasions and other sorts of "licks" are commonplace. He spends much of the rest of the song detailing his everyday experiences in the area, most of which are rooted in illicit activity and precarious situations. He also makes it a point to "shout out" the predominantly low-income African American neighborhoods in the Southwest including his Alief, Missouri City, Sand Piper, Spice Lane, and Bob White.

Neighborhood anthems like Rob Gullatte's "My Side of Town" are key strategies that Houston hip hop artists use to establish their strong identification with their 'hoods. These songs are intended to instill neighborhood pride by featuring lyrics that present place icons in a spirited manner. These songs follow a formula. Local artists of the 1990s established a song-structure formula in which the chorus is derived from the neighborhood name, and the verses take the listener deep into the culture of the neighborhood. One such song is "Cloverland" by the Botany Boyz, from their 1997 album *Thought of Many Ways*.

> Botany is the block that stays crunk at all times
> Nothing but oz's, 50 packs, and small dimes
> At all times a nigga on the cut servin' the fiends
> Tryin' to come big suburban fully loaded with screens

Here, Botany Boyz member Big DEZ offers us a look into the illicit aspect of street life. His opening line, "Botany is the block that stays crunk at all times," marks Botany Lane as the premier social spot of Cloverland and suggests that it is the site of significant illicit activity such as homicides, drug dealing, and robbery. He then details the various activities in which he and his peer group engage. It is important for him to exhibit pride; in addition, it is more important for him to establish a connection between his personal identity and his community identity using neighborhood to do so.

"Mo City Thugz" (2013) is a song and video released by rapper JB in collaboration with Z-Ro from the Screwed Up Click, Lil Flea of Street Military, and crooner Ronnie Spencer, whose R & B stylings have become a staple of the Houston hip hop scene. The song is a tribute to Missouri City, a medium-sized suburb situated in Houston's southwest side. Missouri City is complex because it is composed of both upper- and lower-income neighborhoods.

"Mo City Thugz" is a lyrical testament to street life in one of Houston's most populous suburbs. It features three generations of Missouri City street rappers, each offering proud proclamations of Missouri City's gangsta pedigree. The youngest artist, JB, opens the track by expressing the unbreakable bond between the suburb and his identity:

> Welcome to the mind of a Mo City nigga
> Mo City nigga, gettin' Mo City skrilla
> Mo City killaz on my side when I ride
> Mo City in the Sky, Mo City 'til I die

As a "Mo City nigga," JB not only claims Missouri City as a residence, he also reveals how the suburb's street space informs his sense of self. A "Mo City nigga" is heavily defined by the particularities of the area. This makes sense considering that his social world is housed within the borders of Mo City. It is where he earns money (Mo City skrilla) and it is his primary location of socialization (Mo City killaz on my side). He suggests an almost spiritual connection to community (Mo City in the Sky).

A common theme within the song is the traversal of various predominantly Black streets and neighborhoods within the suburb. JB mentions riding down West Fuqua and hanging out in the Ridgemont 4 neighborhood. Z-Ro, who calls himself the Mo City Don, also cites Ridgemont 4 while also mentioning the street South Post Oaks, a popular pathway connecting Houston and Missouri City. Lil Flea gets more specific:

> From Quail Green West
> To Hunters Glenn Three
> To Briar Gate Duplexes to BGT

References to specific streets and subdivisions serve to lyrically identify the physical spaces and communities that make up the imagined territory. I say "imagined" because the Missouri City described by this trio of rappers does not reflect the social complexity of the suburb. Again, this song is a dedication to Black Missouri City, a smaller, community-determined entity within the larger suburb. No references are made to the upper-income, predominantly White neighborhoods such as Quail Meadow. The predominantly Black neighborhoods of Missouri City, which are in abundance, fall outside of popular conceptions of the city held by those within the Greater Houston metropolis. References to these particular streets and neighborhoods serve to identify where and what Missouri City is within the Black Houston imagination.

Similar to the Botany Boyz in "Cloverland," the artists on "Mo City Thugz" describe the Missouri City way of life. This includes "swangin'" in slabs, hanging with friends, sexual encounters, confronting foes, a little bit of crime, and evading the police. None of this serves to present Missouri City as a unique entity within the complex of Black Houston-area enclaves. That is because, in terms of sheer social practice, Missouri City is not any different from any other Black neighborhood. Missouri City street identity, or being a Mo City nigga, is the convergence of common Houston street practice with bounded place. It is enacting of popular street identity within a particular, well-defined place.

"I'm a Bloc Boy" (2012) by the Bloc Boyz Click takes a different approach. Instead of focusing on a single neighborhood, the song offers a survey of the

Houston 'hoods from which the group members emerge. This song meticulously illuminates and celebrates life in their respective neighborhoods. In this part, Big Be positions himself as a vocal agent for Cloverland, educating the listener on the notable activities and places that define the neighborhood:

Big Body Be Bloc B-o-y-z
Accompanied by bad bitches as far as the eyes see
when it comes to doin' me, It's Clover L-A-N-D
I put the chopper to a nigga head on that Fairgreen

Each prospective member follows a similar format. Big Al raps about selling drugs on Denton Street in the Northside's Lakewood neighborhood:

Den block hustler, Lakewood Click
Set the 'hood on fire way back in '96
Flaggin' down cars in the streets gettin' paid
Nigga dope money bought my first padded leather J's

The song closes with a 'hood "roll call"[1] in which Bloc Boyz members offer shout outs to the city's various Black 'hoods. The accompanying video furthers this dedication to place by showing each member rapping their verses in front of identifiable markers of their neighborhoods. Big Be's scene is set at Cloverland Park. Big Al performs his verse on the corner of the aforementioned Denton Street as well as in front of a shabby store called the Denton Foot Mart. Adrian's verse contains scenes of him rapping outside of the various apartment complexes situated in TABB City. In "I'm a Bloc Boy," the Bloc Boyz Click rep their 'hoods in a plainly spoken yet creatively effective manner.

Neighborhood anthems such as the ones presented here serve to build up the streetwise mythology of the neighborhood, which in turn allows the rap artists to use it as a resource for respect. This process is cyclical and stems from the reciprocal relationship between individual and community. These anthems primarily consist of artists presenting elements of their personal involvement in street life. These individual tales are framed in such a way that they represent the general street dynamics of the neighborhood, building up the potential of the neighborhood. This allows rappers and non-rapping residents to use the neighborhood as cultural capital within the streets and the hip hop scene at large.

Figure 8. Block Boyz Click at the Houston Slab Parade and Family Festival in 2013. Photo by author.

CITY OF SYRUP

Much of the lyrical content written by Houston hip hop artists expresses differential identities as determined by neighborhood. Nevertheless, a central force—the City of Houston itself—unites Houston rappers across neighborhoods. Houston hip hop music exhibits a strong sense of civic pride rooted in the perceived uniqueness of social life within the city. The strong place-identity within local and regional hip hop centers can be attributed, at least in part, to the increased media attention to the ghetto in the mid- to late-1980s, which situated the varying local street spaces in active conversation with one another for the first time. The 'hood was in vogue, and the catalyst was the crack-cocaine scare viewed by many as a national problem affecting a cross section of urban centers. In the following commentary, sociologists Craig Reinarman and Harry G. Levine summarize the "crack scare" that swept across America at the close of the 1980s: "In the spring of 1986, American politicians and news media began an extraordinary antidrug frenzy that ran until 1992. Newspapers, magazines, and television networks regularly carried lurid stories about a new 'epidemic' or 'plague' of drug abuse, especially crack cocaine. They said this 'epidemic' was spreading rapidly from cities to the suburbs and was destroying American society. Politicians from both parties made increasingly strident calls for a 'War on Drugs'" (1997, 1).

During this era, the War On Drugs was fought on 'hood soil. Predominantly Black and Latino inner-city spaces dominated mainstream local and national news with reporting that centered on crack abuse, tales of robbery and homicide, and the social condition of these communities. Such content worked to make Black men the face of social depravity. At the same time, it broke down the discursive isolation of streets around the country. Any young man or woman who knew the streets of Houston was now able to turn on the television and witness the dynamics of the Philadelphia streets. The crack scare placed divergent street spaces in conversation with one another. Economic practices, language, clothing styles, vehicle aesthetics, and other cultural trends were now being shared between geographically distant streets. In a sense, the media helped create a national street space consisting of the disparate but now readily accessible local and regional street space.

The rise of gangsta rap in the late 1980s did much to further the existence of the idea of a nation of streets. As I have previously discussed, territoriality has been a foundational aspect of hip hop culture. Early New York City graffiti writers began creating tags made up of their nickname and street number, and old-school party MCs would reference their 'hoods in shout outs to the crowd. Territoriality became explicit and important with the arrival of gangsta rap. Sociologist Eithne Quinn argues that unique territorial expressions were central to gangsta rappers' commercial success: "Gangsta rap continually elaborated highly appealing and marketable expression of authentic place-bound identity (live from the ghetto)" (2005, 67). Gangsta rap artists such as N.W.A., Ice-T, and Compton's Most Wanted were successful because they were able to market "Compton" as an experience or brand. Subsequent gangsta-based scenes such as Oakland, Miami, Detroit, and Houston followed Compton's model by curating and marketing place-bound identities.

This national street space reflects certain aspects of the local streets. Artists continue to rep their 'hoods by exhibiting strong pride and allegiance to their cities. Houston rappers are explicit about their love for their city and its importance in their art. For instance, local rapper Zavey, who was raised in Southwest Houston, once said to me, "Wherever I go, I'm gon' put on for my city. I'm gon' rep where I'm from" (interview with the author, 2012). Rapper EDF, who grew up in Southside's Hiram Clarke neighborhood, shares his sentiment: "Musically, I can proudly say, if I'm ever on *Rap Fix* one day or if I'm on *106 & Park* [two popular hip hop music video shows], I know the critics are gonna come out and say 'Aw man, that nigga is so Houston'" (interview with the author, June 2012).

Doughbeezy was born in Cleveland, Ohio, but raised in Houston's southeastern suburbs. A Houston Rockets cap, featuring the logo from their mid-1990s National Basketball Association championship years, occupies a prominent position on his 2011 mixtape *Reggie Bush and Kool-Aid*. The placement of the hat, as he tells me, is an intentional representation of civic pride: "The hat was put there on purpose. It's just a little piece that symbolizes where I'm from. I was born in Cleveland, Ohio. That's always my home. But Houston is my home, too. That's the place that raised me. So, I feel like it's my job to hold down the city in any way that I can" (interview with the author, December 2011).

Local artists commonly represent the city through city anthems. These songs work to ingrain pride within the local streets and communicate to others that the Houston streets are worthy of the same respect afforded to other local street spaces. "Welcome to Houston" is a posse cut featuring a number of Houston's most popular emcees including Slim Thug, Paul Wall, Trae, and Bun B. It was released on Slim Thug's 2007 album *Boss of All Bosses*. As a collective, the featured artists seek to present Houston as a unique iteration of hip hop culture. They desire to identify the elements that make Houston unique within the larger hip hop landscape. Bun B, Paul Wall, and Mike Jones call Houston "the city of candy" and the "home of 84s" in reference to slab culture. Paul Wall discusses the city's native drug culture, "where gangsta smoke water / with drank stains on their shirt." Each artist on the song makes reference to particular Houston neighborhoods: Slim Thug represents his Northside, Lil Keke cites Sunny Side and South Park, while Bun B mentions important Houston freeways (US 59, I-45, I-10, and I-610). "Welcome to Houston" features a collective of Houston rap's most cherished artists operating as a unified force, seeking to present their city's sociocultural distinctiveness. The track is a creative declaration of the Houston way of life that allows each individual artist to tap into the commercial potential that comes with such peculiarity.

The Bloc Boyz Click exhibit a different type of civic pride on their 2010 song "Welcome to Screwston." A nickname for the city that emerged in the mid-2000s, "Screwston" reflects local identity informed by street life and the work of early screw artists. It is an image of the city from the street's point of view. On "Welcome to Screwston," the Bloc Boyz provide a primer on the social life in the streets of Houston. Slab culture provides the thematic foundations for the song as they attempt to present Houston as an unparalleled iteration of street culture. The song's chorus, "Let me tell you how we do it down in Houston. We be rollin' on swangas," reveals the Bloc Boyz intend to celebrate the uniqueness of the Houston streets. The first verse is even more illuminating:

> We representin' Houston,
> Plates say Texas
> When them boys see us
> Bet they gon' respect us
> This is Hustle Town
> I wear it on my back
> I keep some fresh kicks
> And some stars on my hat
> When we raise up the trunk
> We gon' show where we at
> Where we reminisce to Screw
> And jam Fat Pat.

The unnamed Bloc Boyz Click rapper literally and figuratively wears Houston, rechristened Hustle Town, on his back via a tattoo. He proudly identifies slabs and the music of deceased S.U.C. members DJ Screw and Fat Pat as markers of Houston's unique identity. His goals are straightforward. He, and other members of the Bloc Boyz Click, proudly represent Houston and demand that others respect its distinctiveness.

Houston artists commonly produce songs that offer their overview of Houston street life and the hip hop scene in efforts to represent their city. At other times, they shift from a focus on cultural space to focusing on the three vernacular artifacts that constitute local hip hop heritage: screw, slabs, and syrup. While some could view their allegiance to screw music as a tribute in itself, screw artists commonly record songs that honor the life and legacy of DJ Screw and the Screwed Up Click. Dat Boi T, a Mexican American rapper from Houston's Second Ward, has released numerous screw tributes, including "Screw Love," "Still a Screwhead," "Nothin' but That Screw," and "Favorite Screw Tape." Others include Bun B's "The Legendary DJ Screw," Macc Grace and Los's "Ol Screws," and VIP's "Old School Screw Tape."

Rapper EDF recorded a particularly compelling screw tribute called "Screw History" (2011). Over a mid-tempo beat and melodic cadence, EDF illuminates DJ Screw and the S.U.C.'s influence on the Houston hip hop culture as well as his personal identity. He opens the song conveying DJ Screw's continued relevance within the Houston hip hop scene:

> Grey tape in the deck
> Tape still movin' slow
> 2010, but we jammin' like its 94.

He then offers a brief but detailed survey of DJ Screw's grey tapes, also known as screwtapes:

> 9 Months Later, Still a G at 23
> Freestyle King, Wreckin' Shop, same ole G
> As of June 27, Southside Still Holdin'
> About two times its been 3 in the Mornin'[2]

Later in the song, he laments the loss of several Screwed Up Click members:

> They say the good die young
> I deal with these losses
> Fat Pat, Big Moe, Dub-K, Big Steve
> Last but not least, DJ Screw
> That was almost the whole D.E.A. crew.[3]

He then offers a definitive statement about the Screwed Up Click's influence on his personal and musical identity.

> It's plain to see
> You can't change E
> The screwed music
> Heavily influenced me.

EDF notes that he recorded "Screw History" to remind listeners of DJ Screw's impact on the Houston scene. "I wanted to put people up on some history," says EDF, whose rap moniker is inspired by S.U.C. member E.S.G. "I wanted to give a remembrance or a dedication to Screw." He also hoped that his memorial of DJ Screw would inspire his hip hop peers: "The reason why I said, 'what would Screw do' [in the chorus] is because I was think man, DJ Screw was always draped out so his body was workin' at half speed but his mind was at one hundred. Screw would still get his ass up to go work on some music. He would get up and go get it. That's a man who died working on music" (interview with the author, June 2012).

EDF reinterprets the popular phrase "What Would Jesus Do" to ask "What Would Screw Do" reflecting the deification of Screw among Houston hip hop artists. DJ Screw's work ethic, which is evidenced by the over two hundred mixtapes he released in his ten-year career, has been a strong influence on EDF. DJ Screw along with the Screwed Up Click left an indelible mark on the local hip hop scene, and EDF wants his generation to aspire to do the same. For EDF and other local artists, DJ Screw is a mark of local excellence. He is a symbol of the genius and prowess that can emerge out of the Houston streets, and as such they celebrate him at every turn.

Artists commonly represent the city by producing songs that celebrate slab culture. These artists continue the legacy of earlier slab anthems such as E.S.G.'s "Swangin' N Bangin'" (1993), Big Mello's "Wegonefunkwichamind" (1994), and Fat Pat's "Tops Drop" (1998). In these slab anthems, artists elucidate slab aesthetics and practice as well as the importance of the culture within the streets. For example, on "Ride on 4s," Northside rapper J-Dawg suggests that slabs can restore civility to the chaotic streets:

> See I's a gangsta nigga
> I'll shoot or shank a nigga
> But there's something 'bout them swangas that'll change a nigga
> Have you chunkin' the deuce up to a stranger nigga

J-Dawg suggests that engaging in slab culture can change one's disposition: from sullen or incensed to affable and easy-going. Instead of threatening others, he chunks up the deuce, a popular non-verbal greeting in the 'hood. J-Dawg speaks to slabs' power to build community. Within the streets, they are a communally defined and locally based symbol of achievement. Slim Thug furthers the notion during his verse on "Ride on 4's":

> H-Town reppin' 'til I'm dead
> From the Trey to the West to the G's off the 'Stead
> Boys out here gettin' bread and reachin' our goals
> Behind tint with the windows closed

For Slim Thug, slabs are tangible symbols of the industrious character of the Houston streets, from Third Ward (Trey) to the Southwest (the West) to Northside's Homestead (Stead). Slabs are rewards for those individuals able to reach their goals in the tempestuous clime of the streets. Other songs including the Bloc Boyz Click's "Officially Ridin Swangas," Killa Kyleon's "Cadillac," and Slim Thug & Z-Ro's "Pokin' Out" convey the same message. These slab anthems reflect the perseverance, diligence, and ingenuity of the Houston streets.

Houston's rise to the mainstream, while brief, left one lasting mark of identity on mainstream hip hop: syrup. Syrup currently stands second only to marijuana as the drug most associated with mainstream hip hop. Many of hip hop's biggest names have appropriated syrup practice. These artists include New York's A$AP Rocky, Toronto's Drake, Atlanta's 2 Chainz, and especially New Orleans's Lil Wayne, who has become the public face of the drug. In an article speculating about the causes of a series of seizures Lil Wayne experienced in 2013, British journalist Andrew Emery of *The Guardian* writes, "While drug experts say its use is now widespread, what's also certain is that the combination originated in Houston, Texas, and is indelibly linked with that city's rich hip-hop culture" (2013).

Syrup remains inextricably tied to Houston hip hop scene because local artists actively reinforce the bond. Through both sonic and visual means, Houston artists have made syrup the most dominant symbol of local identity within the city and around the country.

Local artist Z-Ro, who sometimes calls himself Barre Kelly,[4] along with Lil O offers a dedication to the drug on their 2009 single "Can't Leave Drank Alone." In the song, Z-Ro offers a humorous yet illustrative reflection on his personal relationship with the drug as well as its relevance to local hip hop culture:

> Me and DJ Screw poured up a pint
> On my twenty second birthday
> And that day was a Monday
> But a nigga didn't wake up until Thursday

Z-Ro reminisces about celebrating his twenty-second birthday by drinking syrup with DJ Screw. Later he assumes the identity of the Barre Baby, a nickname used by S.U.C. member Big Moe to convey his love for syrup. Big Moe was the city's chief promulgator of syrup before his death in 2007. By aligning himself with DJ Screw and Big Moe, Z-Ro cites the consumption and promotion of lean as an important part of his identity. Furthermore, he highlights lean's important position within the legacy of the screw movement and the larger Houston hip hop culture.

Other Houston artists support Z-Ro's conflation of screw, syrup, and local identity. Doughbeezy, who has dedicated many lines to his penchant for weed, notes, "I definitely do lean because it's something that I seen growing up. When you saw the slab, you also saw the two cups in the cup holder. It was a part of the screw lifestyle or the culture that he created" (interview with the author, December 2011).

Doughbeezy performs on "Danny Glover," a song that also features fellow Houston artists Maxo Kream and Short Dawg. Maxo Kream is a young rapper from Southwest Houston who has built a major following through a series of well-received mixtapes. His verse on the song offers insight into lean's function as a marker of identity, but also the complexities of the drug on the Houston streets:

> Sip an eight and a two liter
> I can't stay awake
> You can catch me on lean
> like I don't have no needs

Maxo Kream exhibits a strong penchant for syrup in his verse. He raps about drinking so much syrup that he can't function, drinking directly out of the codeine bottle, and consuming his brother's whole stash. He even prefers to mix his syrup with blue soda, reflecting his membership in the Crips street gang, whose color is blue. While these lines are humorous, the second half of this verse highlights the illicitness of the drug. He notes that "selling Karo get a fuck nigga killed." On the streets, syrup dealers commonly "cut" or dilute codeine cough syrup with corn syrup such as Karo (Whitfield 2008). This enables them to sell more product. However, syrup drinkers can easily detect diluted syrup. Considering the high retail price, which is between 300 and 500 dollars a pint, consumers become understandably vexed by this perceived deception. Cutting syrup with corn syrup can, as Maxo Kream notes, cost a dealer his life. Houston artists understand that syrup has a sinister side but continue to actively promote it in their music.

Houston has become known as "The City of Syrup" due to the thematic prominence of the drug in local rap music and videos. It is a nickname that has become a staple of local rap lyricism. "The City of Syrup," however, is more than a syrup-infused moniker. It is a creative reimagining of Houston, rooted in the streets and the hip hop scene. It is a Houston where street values and practices are normative. It represents a locale where sipping cough syrup, riding slab, and listening to slow music are ordinary practices. "The City of Syrup," similar to Parliament's "Chocolate City," finds a socioculturally dominated African American citizenry discursively reorganizing the power structure within their city.

This nickname for Houston first rose to the public's attention via Big Moe's aptly titled 2000 album *The City of Syrup*. Living up to its title, the album was an amalgamation of everything that defined Houston's street culture as illustrated on the album's lead single, "Barre Baby." On the surface, this song merely appears to be dedicated to the favorite concoction of Moe and the Screwed Up Click. A deeper analysis, however, reveals that it positions syrup or lean as a symbolic index of the entire subculture. Big Moe's love for syrup, expressed via the chorus, acts as the thematic frame through which Moe offers a survey of Southside practice. His checklist for Houston hip hop identity includes wearing Versace ('sache) sunglasses, riding slab, sporting bald-fade haircuts, and of course, sipping syrup. His vocals are relaxed and nonchalant, which brings an air of routine or normalcy. It suggests that these elements listed are not at all exceptional, rather, they are commonplace for anyone who embraces local hip hop identity. The final line of the song feeds right into the chorus on which Big Moe defines himself as the "Barre Baby." In short, all of these practices are embodied by his Barre Baby identity. "Barre Baby" is Big Moe's specific articulation of Houston hip hop identity.

Along with the lyrical content, Big Moe's *City of Syrup* is important from a visual standpoint. The album's front cover features the image of larger-than-life Big Moe pouring purple liquid (assumed to be lean) out of a white cup onto the Houston skyline. Above this image is Big Moe's name spelled out in Old English lettering with a purple fill. This album cover sparked the initial association of the color purple with Houston hip hop identity. It has come to symbolize a unified Houston hip hop scene that features common attitudes, practices, and approaches to music making. Through practices of local hip hop artists and fans, the color purple has become a primary marker of Houston identity both locally and nationally.

Since Big Moe's *City of Syrup*, Houston hip hoppers have actively reinforced the relationship between syrup, the color purple, and Houston hip hop identity. Killa Kyleon produced a series of mixtapes called *Purple Punch*. Maxo Kream's *Purple Strikes* and Lil Ray's *Purple Tape* are among the many local screwed and chopped albums that mention purple in the title or feature purple as a prominent color in the cover art. Screwed-and-chopped remixes of non-local music receive a similar treatment. The color is also popular in local hip hop–related fashion and visual art.

Hip hop artists outside of Houston also reference the color in their song titles and lyrics in their appropriation of Houston's screw style. A$AP Rocky, a native of Harlem, NY, is an artist who has adopted elements of Houston's hip hop subculture as evidenced by his 2011 single, "Purple Swag." The beat, produced by A$AP Mob producer Ty Beats, samples "Still Tippin'," the iconic song by Houston artists Slim Thug, Paul Wall, and Chamillionaire released in 2004. Though a relatively short track, several lines contain explicit Houston symbols. The mention of "candy cars" in the third line of the first verse and the phrases "that paint drip" and "I still tip" are all references to slab culture. "I'm coming down," also mentioned in the first verse, is a popular line that Houston rappers use during freestyles. The Houston references are even more direct in the sixth line of the second verse. "Trill" is a phrase that originated with Port Arthur, Texas, group UGK and has become popular within the Houston rap scene. A portmanteau of "true" and "real," *trill* has become a popular way Texas hip hoppers identify themselves. When A$AP Rocky says that he's "Texas trill," he points directly to the Texas influence on his identity. He subsequently qualifies this, by saying that "in NY we spit it slow," suggesting that his expression of Houston identity is a rearticulation shaped by his New York origins. This rearticulation is also supported by the video, which features a multiracial group of fashion-forward hipster youth, drinking 40z, smoking marijuana, and wearing grills. The overall scene reflects a type of flashiness that has long been a characteristic of Harlem hip hop, as evidenced by Big L, Cam'ron, and P. Diddy. The song title and other Houston identity markers referenced in "Purple Swag" represent a fusion of Houston and Harlem hip hop identities.

Cultural identity is the linchpin of Houston's hip hop scene as it has fueled its social, structural, and commercial viability. For these reasons, as local artist D-Risha notes, "Houston is real, real protective of its culture" (interview with the author, 2011). While some locals have embraced A$AP Rocky, his appropriation of Houston identity has riled others, like rappers Carter and Marcus Manchild as well as producer Mike Dean (Samuel 2012; Markman 2012). As self-exalted representatives of Houston's hip hop culture, the Bloc Boyz Click remixed "Purple Swag" (2012) as reclamation of a local identity distorted by a New York–based artist seeking mainstream relevance. The Bloc Boyz Click, over a reformulated beat by group member Lil Kano, presents syrup and the color purple as a symbol of the entire scene. The song's hook makes the most explicit connection between syrup consumption and local identity:

> H-Town we sip that purple, we want to smoke that purple all the way to NY
> We got 'em sippin purple, We got 'em sippin' purple
> Houston, Texas Southside

In his verse, Bloc Boyz Click member Dunta establishes Houston as syrup's place of origin and elucidates other core aspects of local scene identity:

> This is H-Town, home of drank people
> Four and a Sprite, that's a purple liter[5]
> Candy paint, chrome grill
> Stash spot for me to hide the heater

Other verses follow this pattern. Each member makes it a point to establish Houston as the birthplace of syrup and to present other core components of local street and hip hop identity, most notably slabs and screw.

The associated music video also reinforces the association between syrup and Houston identity. The opening scene of the video features a foregrounded Will Lean rapping his lead vocals. Behind him are a dozen other individuals, including members of the Bloc Boyz Click, throwing up various signs, including the one that represents Houston. This is not a scene uncommon to rap videos, as it is in accordance with the communal nature of hip hop culture. What makes the scene unique is the purple tint that overlays the video footage. This purple tint appears throughout the video. At times, like in this opening scene, the color is deep enough to add a purplish hue to the rappers' brown skin. At other points it is much lighter, only detectable when juxtaposed with a white background. Furthermore, several members of the group are wearing purple articles of clothing. As a symbol of Houston identity, the prominence of purple in the video works to associate the social activities depicted in the video with Houston street culture.

The video also features other, more material representations of syrup identity including double white cups and Sprite bottles. In Houston's hip hop culture, syrup is often consumed out of two Styrofoam cups. The double cups used by many Houston rap artists, as well as major national acts such as Lil Wayne and Drake, has come to symbolize the consumption of lean (Reid 2008). Similarly, Sprite is a popular mixer for syrup. The codeine/promethazine is poured into a bottle of Sprite, along with jolly ranchers, and shaking the bottle up mixes the entire concoction. The presence of these symbols of syrup is supported by symbols of Houston identity such as Houston Astros baseball hats and Houston-related T-shirts. Ultimately, through these pieces of material culture, the Bloc Boyz reinforce the conflation of syrup consumption and Houston identity.

When I asked group member Adrian about their motivations for remixing the track, he said, "We did our version because, if our culture is going to be used, we need to speak on it on our terms. So people know how it is coming from people who are actually dwelling in the south. Not to take anything away from A$AP Rocky. It was a good cut, a good album and everything. We just felt that it would be more official or more solid if we did our version" (interview with the author, April 2012). While generally laudatory, Adrian's comments suggest that his group and other Houston artists claim ownership of the cultural artifacts used by A$AP Rocky. In addition, he feels that Rocky's track is an inauthentic expression of Houston identity. So Adrian and the Bloc Boyz Click responded by giving the world an official presentation of these icons, "official" meaning one grounded in Houston experience.

For the Bloc Boyz Click, "Purple Swag" is much more than a generic piece of hip hop slang. Contained in that single phrase are the people, practices, places, and experiences that define Houston's indigenous hip hop culture. Screwed Up Click member Lil Randy notes:

> That's our identity. I mean, you can't knock it. I don't glorify drinking syrup, but that is our identity. We weren't intentionally trying to tell the world to drink syrup, but they did it, you know what I'm saying. That's just a part of our identity. It's almost like getting shot in the shoulder. You get shot in the shoulder, you can't remove that mark. That's a part of your identity. You don't like the scar. You wish the scar was gone, but it's a scar that's there and it is what it is. Houston music is the City of Syrup. That's our culture. (Interview with the author, April 2012)

Although identification through color is neither a fundamental nor common social practice within hip hop, the color purple has come to symbolize the idiosyncratic execution of the art form within the city's borders. "Purple

Swag" is a color-coded articulation of Houston hip hop experience that serves
to define the disparate factions of Houston hip hop culture as a collective,
affording them a distinctive place within the larger hip hop landscape.

HOOD CHECK

For Houston artists, "reppin' your 'hood" goes beyond the field of recording.
Local rap artists represent their 'hoods during live performances as well. I attended many types of performances while conducting fieldwork in Houston,
including concerts, block parties, CD release parties, and showcases. "Reppin'
your 'hood" took place at every turn. The Action Smoke Shop block party held
on May 27, 2012, provides a particularly compelling example of this practice.

The Action Smoke Shop and Studio is located at the northern end of a
strip center on Cullen Boulevard in the South Side. It is a space marked by
a neon sign that reads "Action" in blue lettering and "Smoke Shop & Studio"
below it in red. It is primarily a smoke shop, so various pipes, bongs, rolling papers, and other materials relating to smoking tobacco or marijuana
dominate its interior. They also sell CDs, films, T-shirts, and other items
related to the local hip hop scene. The recording studio occupies the back
of the premises, separated from the main retail space. The Action Smoke
Shop is owned and operated by members of 3-4 Action, a subgroup of the
Screwed Up Click whose membership dates back to Screw's earliest mixtapes.
3-4 Action commissioned its own DJ Screw tape, simply called *3-4 Action*,
which features a freestyle by member Poppy along with the late Pimp C of
Underground Kingz (UGK). Reflecting their membership in the S.U.C., the
Action Smoke Shop is also known as "The House that Screw Built." A mural
of Screw adorns one of the interior walls, and below the exterior shop sign
is a smaller sign that reads "Home of the SUC and 34 Action Family."

The block party was a free event held in the strip center's parking lot. No
tickets were required and people were free to come and go as they pleased.
Nevertheless, the crowd size was around three hundred at its peak and never
seemed to move significantly beyond or below that. In terms of demographics, the audience was predominantly African American, but there was a significant Hispanic contingent. There appeared to be an equal amount of men
and women of all ages.

The performance lineup featured a "who's who" of the Houston rap scene. E.S.G., Lil O, and Lil Keke of the Screwed Up Click performed, as did Killa Kyleon and J-Dawg, who were both members of Slim Thug's Boss Hogg Outlawz group at one point. There were also several up-and-coming local rappers, most notably Bleeda from Southwest Houston.

Every single artist that graced the stage that day represented their 'hoods in either a minor or major way. These displays of territorial allegiance and identity were met with roaring affirmation from the largely Southside crowd. For example, Lil Keke introduced his 1996 single "Southside," itself a strong territorial statement, with the following lines: "Herschelwood's my motherfuckin' block. Put your H's up if you know what it is." Lil Keke reps the Herschelwood section of South Park and told Herschelwood-based audience members to project the "H" hand sign to represent along with him. Lil O, from Southwest Houston, took a similar approach as he introduced his song "Can't Leave Drank Alone" when he said, "Southwest! Dubs-up, I see ya!" Both Lil O and Lil Keke repped the 'hood in a fairly modest way and drew strong reactions from the crowd.

Compared to Lil Keke and Lil O, Killa Kyleon repped his Dead End South Park 'hood in a much more elaborate way:

> I gotta do a 'hood check right quick my nigga. Where Dead End at in the motherfucka? Everybody reppin' Dead End put a hand up high. We see them Bank-boys in this motherfucka. What it do? Yeah, I see them niggas. Chrystal Springs, the Villas, Kennedy Heights, Hillwood and all that shit.
> [moves into rapped segment]
> Dead End. D-E-A-D my nigga
> Where the streets are closed.
> Pimps, players, ballers, and even CEOs
> [moves out of rapped segment]
> You heard of that? That's what we rep.

Kyleon offered what he called a "'hood check," a public statement of recognition and dedication to Dead End residents in the crowd. As part of this 'hood check, Kyleon recognized Dead End apartment complexes (Chrystal Springs and the Villas) and adjacent neighborhoods (South Bank, Kennedy Heights, and Hillwood). Audience members from these areas returned with roaring applause and cheers. Kyleon's ability to survey the crowd and identify the

Figure 9. Killa Kyleon performance at Action Smoke Shop block party on May 27, 2012. Photo by author.

specific South Park–area 'hoods in attendance shows that he has an intimate knowledge of his 'hood. He also offered a short rapped segment that characterizes Dead End street life. He closed by saying "that's what we represent," declaring that even amongst residents from other neighborhoods who may hold some animosity toward them, he proudly represents "Dead End" for both himself and others in the crowd.

J-Dawg's performance is particularly compelling as it shows that artists must negotiate their approaches to reppin' the 'hood as they navigate different spaces around the city. J-Dawg, who is from Northside's Acres Homes, was among Swishahouse's first artists and has released several well-received solo and group album over the years. Whereas other artists explicitly represented specific neighborhoods, J-Dawg made his only expression of territorial identity at the opening of his set when he said, "We rep the whole Houston, the whole 360." As a Northside-based rapper performing at a Southside establishment and in front of a Southside audience, who proudly repped their 'hoods, J-Dawg may have felt that such an expression of Northside identity would cause him to lose the crowd. However, it may have been a humanitarian effort. J-Dawg, while one of Houston's most respected street artists, projected strong altruistic sensibilities throughout his performance. For example, he is a self-proclaimed Crip, but at one point he gave a shout out to all of the various gangs represented in the audience—including the Bloods, Vice Lords, and Folks Nation as well as the Crips—and told them to rep their sets in unison. He also made a point, on multiple occasions, to convey his bond with another performer who was a Blood gang member from Southwest Houston. J-Dawg's behavior suggests that he understands the power of the "hood check," and to vociferously rep the Northside at a Southside event could possibly incite territorial tensions among the audience. His performance demonstrates that repping your 'hood is not a reflexive measure but rather one that involves contemplation and negotiation.

SHOWING FACE IN THE HOOD

Properly reppin' the 'hood takes more than making songs about your neighborhood, however. As rapper Big Be told me, "You gotta do more for your 'hood than throw it up or jump some niggas at a club" (interview with the author, April 2012). Artists must "show face," or maintain a consistent physical presence in their 'hoods. The Bloc Boyz consistently show face as their headquarters is the garage of a single-family home on the infamous Botany Lane in Cloverland. Group manager OG Scott says that he maintains the studio in Cloverland in order to "stay connected to the streets." Furthermore, the group makes it a point to give back to the 'hoods that raised them. The Bloc Boyz Click gives back to the neighborhood by holding Easter egg hunts and Christmas toy drives at nearby Cloverland Park every year.

Local rappers also make it a point to make appearances at important community events, especially those centered on issues that acutely affect the Black working class. For example, rapper Bun B of UGK and DJ Michael Watts were present at the 3rd Annual Pimp C Health and Wellness Fair, an event that I attended, held at the Fifth Ward Multi-service center on December 7, 2011. The event was held in honor of the late rapper/producer Pimp C, who died on December 4, 2007, from a combination of sleep apnea and overdose of promethazine-codeine syrup. Attendees received free HIV testing, immunizations, and routine physical exams as well as general health and wellness information. Additionally, I witnessed rappers Trae tha Truth, Bun B, Slim

Thug, Scarface, and Willie D address the crowd at the Trayvon Martin Community Rally and Prayer held at Emancipation Park on March 25, 2012. The event was held to honor the life of Trayvon Martin and protest his death. Martin was a seventeen-year-old Black male Floridian who was killed during an encounter with George Zimmerman, a voluntary neighborhood watchman (Horwitz 2012). Rappers took turns on the mic, each calling for justice for Trayvon while also urging the community to seek solutions to problems of police harassment and Black-on-Black violence. Rap artists in Houston attribute much of their success to their 'hoods and feel an obligation to give back wherever they can. For them, reppin' the 'hood means to shout out and show face, but also to stand up for their 'hoods at every turn.

As I have shown, Houston street artists actively represent their 'hoods—specific neighborhoods, parts of town, or the entire city itself—through both recordings and live performances. On their records, artists represent by proudly depicting their 'hood's street acumen and by honoring the various elements that mark the screw tradition. During live performances, artists represent by making strong declarative statements that convey their unwavering association with their particular 'hoods.

Reppin' the 'hood is important for local street artists from a commercial standpoint. Showing allegiance to the neighborhood can directly impact a rapper's status and success within the hip hop scene. "The streets is home," Dunta told me. "If you ain't got your 'hood or the streets behind you, you're gonna eventually fall off. It don't matter who you is, everybody is gonna get back to your roots and ask those questions" (interview with the author, April 2012). Doughbeezy's career trajectory is a particularly informative example of this. Doughbeezy was raised in Southeast Houston, an area made up of several sizable suburbs. He tirelessly represents the Southeast in his music, and he even calls himself the Southeast Beast. Regarding his vocal devotions to Southeast Houston, Doughbeezy conveyed to me, "If I don't do it [represent the Southeast], who else will? You feel what I'm sayin'? I think its real important that it's known that without the Southeast, and the people that know me personally, without them, I wouldn't be where I'm at" (interview with the author, December 2011).

Doughbeezy is certainly earnest regarding his desires for people to understand how the Southeast has impacted him. However, his steadfast dedication has greatly paid off, as he relates in the following comments: "I started to get my buzz at the shows. And, at my shows, it would be fifty plus people coming to the shows from my area. People I've known and people that I didn't know, but they knew someone who knew me and heard my music. So, them coming to the shows and singing my words, that's what really started my buzz. So, I think its real important to represent where I'm from and hold it down for them, like they held me down" (interview with the author, December 2011).

The Southeast community supports Doughbeezy by attending his concerts in droves because he represents them on the public stage. Fellow local rapper D-Risha supports Doughbeezy's assertion when he says, "Doughbeezy's whole Southeast come to his shows like forty or fifty deep. It's given him a real buzz" (interview with the author, November 2011). Representin' for the Southeast as well as the city has given Doughbeezy a high amount of cultural capital, which he has exchanged for critical and commercial success. Rappers' spatial-specificity raises their level of respect within a local scene fueled by active audiences who desire locally identified music.

Reppin' your 'hood also has a practical function for local hip hop artists. Street artists remain inextricably tied to street culture. The hip hop scene and the streets commonly intersect at various locations in the 'hood, most notably in clubs where rappers perform and street figures socialize. Because of this, the specter of violence is ceaseless within the scene. During my time in the field, the Houston hip hop scene was rocked by several violent incidents that illuminated the relationship between the streets and the local hip hop scene. On November 25, 2011, Dominic "Money Clip-D" Brown, a member of rapper Trae tha Truth's Assholes By Nature crew, was murdered as he sat in his car outside of Breakers, an after-hours club in Southwest Houston (Stanton 2011). Money Clip-D was a beloved figure within the scene and many artists and fans mourned his death. Almost a month later, the Assholes By Nature performed at local venue Warehouse Live and each member wore jackets that read "RIP Money Clip-D ABN 4_Life" on the back. Before the scene could properly heal, on May 3, 2012, Screwed Up Click rapper D-Pac, also known as Lil Dex, was killed while attending a candlelight vigil held in honor of a recent murder victim at George T. Nelson Park in the Southside (Kobza 2012). A second Assholes By Nature–related shooting occurred on June 20, 2012, at High Rollers strip club. This incident, which occurred after a Trae tha Truth performance at the club, left the rapper wounded and fellow ABN members Dinky D and Poppa C dead (Warren 2012). These violent episodes were merely the latest within a community that has lost luminaries such as brothers Fat Pat and Big Hawk along with Big Steve to gun violence. Because they navigate street spaces, rap artists are beholden to its cultural dynamics, namely, the acquisition of respect as a deterrent to corporeal vulnerability. Similar to other street occupants, rap artists rep their 'hoods as a way to improve their respect and lessen the possibility of harm. However, as the previous examples demonstrate, these measures are not always successful.

Many local artists rep their 'hoods out of a sense of responsibility. They understand the power of their voices and want to use it to affirm and uplift their communities. According to Michael P. Jeffries, such territorial narratives "open the possibility of new productive and prideful identities" in the 'hood (Jeffries 2011, 64). Local rappers feel that they instill pride by making their 'hood popular or "putting their 'hood on the map." MC Cl'Che from South Park says, "I want to bring my community up with me. So if I'm popular, then my community is popular" (interview with the author, December 2011). Hiram Clarke native EDF concurs with her when he tells me that "your 'hood is only as popular as you" (interview with the author, 2012). In addition, rappers also rep their 'hoods in order to improve the material conditions of their 'hoods. As Cl'Che once told me, "If I rep my 'hood, then all of these small businesses and other people doing things are going to get more business" (interview with the author, December 2011).

Reppin' the 'hood is mutually beneficial for rappers and their communities. I witnessed this phenomenon when I interviewed rapper E.S.G. on March 9, 2012. He accepted my interview request with a single text message that read "come to the 'hood" accompanied by an address for a Southside residence. When I arrived at the address that March afternoon, I found E.S.G. along with several other African American men joyously fraternizing under the carport of a modest single-family house. E.S.G. informed me that the home belongs to a friend of his and that it is one of his primary hangout spots. I interviewed E.S.G. while his friend continued their informal party. Over the course of our conversation, other individuals arrived at the house to converse with E.S.G. along with the other men present. Many others greeted the rapper as they passed down the street in their cars. E.S.G. responded to every salutation in a genuinely affable manner, showing that he was sincerely appreciative of his relationship with his 'hood community. As I witnessed E.S.G. socialize that afternoon, I realized that for many artists, reppin' the 'hood is more intrinsic than strategic. E.S.G. is a local legend whose music has influenced artists far beyond his local scene. He has garnered enough success and earned enough money that he could easily dissociate himself from the working-class experience and enjoy an unbothered life of privilege. However, he continues to not only represent but experience the 'hood because, as he told me, "it is in his heart." The sites, attitudes, practices, and peoples that constitute his 'hood are part of his selfhood. The place-defined socialization of his youth and young adulthood produced who he is today: a rap artist, friend, husband, and father. His Screwed Up Click crewmate Big Pokey shared a similar feeling to me when he said that "the 'hood raised me." Their personal successes are part of the collective effort of his fellow community members and as such, the community has a vested interest in them. Rappers such as E.S.G., Big Pokey, Rob Gullatte, the Bloc Boyz Click, and others rep' the 'hoods as a way to allow the community to share in their successes and reap the rewards of their communal investment.

5

TURNIN' HEADZ

It's like family, you have aunts and uncles that you're
not close to or you don't relate to. But at the end of the day,
they are still your family and still your blood.
And they still make up who you are.

—Nasty Nique Roots

Check Other Outfitters was a multifaceted boutique on the corner of Bagby and McGowan streets in Houston's midtown district, formerly part of the Fourth Ward. Between 2010 and 2012, the store was firmly situated in a newly built strip center, nestled between an Italian restaurant to the left and a coffee shop to the right. Founded by local hip hop producer Tommy Bumps, it was a hip hop–related emporium of sorts. The store sold T-shirts, shoes, and hats by contemporary brands such as Herschel Supply, Bathing Ape, and Supreme to teen and young adult hip hop clientele. It carried hip hop–related literature, artwork, and music. Along with SF2 and Premium Goods, it was one of several new Houston-area stores geared toward this burgeoning consumer base.

On the first Thursday of every month, the store transformed itself from a retail space to a performance site for Turnin' Headz: Blank Canvas, a hip hop showcase. Turnin' Headz was the brainchild of That Purple Bastard, a local hip hop producer and entrepreneur, who envisioned a space for young emcees to test their skills in front of a supportive audience. Renzo and Ensane, two local emcees, hosted the show.

Upon first entering Check Other Outfitters on Thursday, November 11, 2011, I realized that the Turnin' Headz community differed radically from my prior conception of Houston hip hop. The audience consisted of a racially diverse group of fashion-forward young adults, and about half appeared to be artists themselves. Musically, the collective of performers had much stylistic variation. Evak, the opener, was a White emcee whose lyrically dense vocal style was reminiscent of that of popular avant-garde rapper Aesop Rock.[1] African American artists J-Stringz and Karo followed Evak, and both performed in a more traditionally Houston-style manner. African American rapper Koby closed the show with aggressively executed punch lines, which were both sharp and smooth.

Despite these stylistic divergences, Houston's hip hop identity was strongly championed but articulated in an alternative style. Each performer made an explicit reference to local hip hop culture, including multiple allusions to screw music and syrup. In addition, artists and many audience members were wearing apparel that featured some reference to Houston. Houston Astros baseball hats and Houston Rockets basketball hats littered the crowd. Stylized depictions of DJ Screw's image, syrup-filled cups, and the word *Houston* were emblazoned on T-shirts. By the end of the night, I understood that while the underground community in Houston is characterized by stylistic variety, it remains rooted in Houston's localized hip hop identity.

The network of audience, artists, and institutions that constitute the Houston hip hop scene have shaped the definition of what it means to be a Houston hip hop artist—representing 'hoods, making lyrical references to lean and slabs, and having a musical grounding in the screw sound—thereby engaging in a form of musical boundary-work. A large number of local artists work within the core of this boundary, including the scene's most popular figures. Local fans crave screw music and it is therefore consistently played in clubs and on terrestrial and internet radio stations.

Turning Headz presents artists whose styles straddle the borders of the Houston hip hop heritage. These artists are greatly influenced by nonlocal influences and a desire to express individual innovations. This segment of the scene is diverse in regard to both race and class. Their aesthetic and cultural divergence from the mean causes them to struggle to maintain relevance within the scene. These artists have labeled their particular community "underground" in reference to larger hip hop trends, but also to reflect their subordinate position within the scene.

HIP HOP IS FOR EVERYONE

Craig "B-Boy Craig" Long is very much the lifeblood of Houston's underground. Every single interview with an underground artist ended with them telling me to go talk to Craig Long. This makes sense considering his long and varied experiences within the local hip hop scene. For Craig, "B-Boy" is not a nickname but an earned title. He's been active in the Houston hip hop scene since the mid-1980s. He started out, appropriately, as a b-boy, performing and competing with friends at Reagan High School in the First Ward. In the late 1980s and early 1990s, He helped build the Houston hip hop scene right alongside artists of larger stature. Since then, he's served the local hip hop community as a deejay, designer, party promoter, historian, and general sage. His effervescent personality and big smile make you feel welcomed within the scene, no matter where you come from or how you come to it.

"That's why my brand is HHIFE. It's Houston Hip Hop Is For Everyone," he tells me from his sister's house in Houston. "It is my goal to make sure people know that when they come to Houston, it's not just this certain type of music" (Craig "B-Boy Craig" Long, interview with the author, 2022). HHIFE is Long's personal brand, but it reflects the collective ethos of Houston's underground hip hop community. It is a statement that highlights the incredible diversity within the local hip hop scene while also critiquing the marginalization of artists whose style diverges from the city's sonic heritage.

For Houston artists, the label *underground* refers to particular experiences on the margin of the Houston hip hop scene, but it connects them to a larger movement. The concept of underground hip hop has a dualistic definition that posits that it is a response to industrial and aesthetic practices of mainstream hip hop. In *Hip Hop Underground: The Integrity and Ethics of Racial Imagination*, Anthony Kwame Harrison interprets its emergence as a result of industrial and ideological concerns:

> Against the commercial ascendance of Music Industry rap, during the mid-to-late-nineties a specific subgenre known as "underground hip hop" developed through networks of Do-It-Yourself (DIY) artists/entrepreneurs, home-based industries, and locally-focused collective movements. While underground hip hop's emergence can be presented as the simultaneous appearance of several (seemingly distinct) local scenes, the widespread practice of spotlighting commercial rap music's inauthenticity as a means of making counter-authenticity claims, coupled with underground hip hop's early utilization of translocal communication channels (most notably the internet), lead me to represent its emergence here as a single countercultural development. (2009, 29)

Underground hip hop, as Harrison notes, is both a network of scenes that operate outside of the mainstream music industry and a type of musical ideology that serves as a counternarrative to mainstream styles.

Underground hip hop in Houston exhibits a cornucopia of styles. Self-proclaimed underground artists include D-Risha, who is heavily influenced by the New York boom-bap[2] and the Memphis horrorcore[3] sounds. Nasty Nique Roots uses a variety of unorthodox rhyme schemes and vocal styles to detail his experiences growing up in Southwest Houston. The Aspiring Me is the son of the late Big Mello of the Screwed Up Click, and his music has a strong bohemian vibe, which inspires self-reflection. Bishop Black is a dynamic artist who uses an aggressive flow to deliver his intricate rhymes. D-Risha, Nasty Nique Roots, The Aspiring Me, and Bishop Black are members of an underground collective that values ingenuity over allegiance to local tradition.

Houston's underground sector exhibits much more racial and gender diversity than its street counterpart. It is dominated by Black male artists and has a growing segment of Hispanic male artists. However, the underground features a sizeable body of White artists, including producer That Purple Bastard and emcees Kyle Hubbard and Thorogood Wordsmith. According to Harrison, the racial demographics of Houston's underground community reflects larger trends: "the emergence of the underground hip hop subgenre offered opportunities for hip hop music production to middle-class, non-urban, non-black male consumers with artistic ambitions and inclinations" (2009, 33). He adds that "underground hip hop's DIY mantra tipped the scales of participation toward those who could best access the specific technologies and financial resources necessary to create and release music on their own" (33). Similar to the borders of underground hip hop communities around the country, the borders of Houston's hip hop production are open to middle-class White kids who have the financial means to produce and release recordings without the backing of major labels. Female participation continues to be limited, but female emcees occupy much more prominent positions in the underground than in the street world. Lyric Michelle, Uzoy, and Genesis Blu are among the underground female rap artists who have received much critical acclaim and have a large following in Houston.

The marginal position of underground hip hoppers is the product of the boundary-work conducted within the Houston hip hop scene. According to ethnomusicologist Marc Gidal, musical boundary-work denotes "the creation, interpretation, and use of music to reinforce, bridge, or reshape boundaries for social, spiritual, political, or other purposes" (2014, 85). Such boundary-work is fundamental to any musical community, according to ethnomusicologist Kay Kaufman Shelemay, who notes, "Musical communities provide particularly striking case studies of processes of boundary formation since specific musical styles can lead the way in either closing off a community or in opening it up to outsiders" (2011, 379). To be a culturally legitimate Houston hip hopper, artists must, to some extent, embrace the four pillars of the scene: screw music, slabs, lean, and reppin' the 'hood. This boundary separates "us" from "them," with "them" being both mainstream Houstonians and other national hip hop centers. It shapes and reinforces a cultural identity that symbolically endows artists and audiences with a strong sense of empowering distinctiveness.

Musical boundaries are more sliding scales than inflexible borders. As such, the most relevant and respected artists within Houston's hip hop scene are therefore those who strongly adhere to the screw identity. Screw-era artists, such as Slim Thug, Z-Ro, and Paul Wall, continue to be the most lauded performers within the scene. Screw-centered upstarts Doughbeezy, Propain, and Kirko Bangz were among the most buzzworthy newcomers during my time in the field. Styles get increasingly less relevant or popular among audiences as they pull away from the core. The greater the amount of individual innovation or diversity of influence, the more a given music is pushed toward the periphery of the community. Underground artists' commitment to stylistic distinctiveness moves them away from the screw tradition and thereby causes their musical products to have low cultural resonance, which in turn situates them in the margins of Houston's hip hop music scene.

Because of their peripheral position, underground artists struggle to commercialize their music, whether through sales of recordings or paid performances. Most Houston-based underground hip hop artists could be considered semiprofessional musicians. Artists work day jobs to support themselves and their musical activities. During my time in the field, D-Risha worked in the stock department at the Puma sneaker store in Houston's Galleria Mall. Nasty Nique Roots was employed as a waiter at local Star Pizza. Both That Purple Bastard and The Aspiring Me worked at a Whole Foods grocery store. While having full-time traditional occupations, these artists do not view music as a hobby: they take their art seriously and invest significant portions of their income into their musical careers.

Cultural and commercial viability requires a constant interaction with local hip hop tradition. Such engagement allows underground artists to move closer to the cultural core of the scene. Underground artists engage with local hip hop cultural identity in a multitude of ways. Some artists make explicit overtures to Houston hip hop identity; others are much subtler. In the following section, I examine how three underground artists, D-Risha, Nasty Nique Roots, and That Purple Bastard, musically resolve local identity with idiosyncratic innovation, creating complex musical products that simultaneously appeal to multiple audiences.

NeGOTIaTInG Space: THRee case STuDIes

D-Risha, Nasty Nique Roots, and That Purple Bastard are three young artists who are active within Houston's hip hop underground. Along with several other rappers, they are members of the Rogue Scholars Alliance (RSA), a loose-knit group that often performs and records together. Each artist takes a unique approach to hip hop music. D-Risha has an aggressive vocal delivery, along with lyrics rooted in battle and life stories. Nasty Nique Roots has a lyrically dense, avant-garde vocal style. That Purple Bastard is a producer whose beats are heavily influenced by psychedelic rock and electronica. Though their styles are vastly different, each artist occupies the same subordinate space within the Houston hip hop scene. They attempt to combat this cultural marginalization through strategic lyrical and instrumental overtures to Houston hip hop tradition. In the following case studies, I examine the ways they negotiate local expectations with individual artistic impulses.

The local elements of the sounds of local underground artists commonly reflect musical enculturation, the natural result of living in and socializing in a space that has a distinct musical identity. "We were all raised on Screw," Nasty Nique told me when I asked him about the influence of screw on his work. "People from our era was raised on that music. Even if we identify with other forms of hip hop more, or even if other forms permeate our music more, that is still the core." For Nasty Nique and other underground artists, DJ Screw remains a revered father-figure, despite their stylistic variation.

That Purple Bastard's music exemplifies this type of musical enculturation. A key musical and industrial force in the underground, he does not fit the stereotype of a Houston hip hop artist. He is White, tall, and rail thin. He sports a bald head and a long, sweeping beard—which, to me, makes him look like he should be playing lead guitar in a post–ZZ Top metal band rather than laying the sonic foundations for a hardcore hip hop crew because of that signature look. Nevertheless, he creates dynamic beats, which can either accompany a rap vocal or be enjoyed on their own as instrumentals.

Purple Bastard's multifaceted musical identity can be attributed to his dynamic personal background. He was born in the Houston suburb of Pasadena, Texas, and raised in a working-class, predominantly Mexican American neighborhood in Southeast Houston. As a child, he spent significant time in the predominantly Black Fifth Ward, having a best friend who stayed in the area. Notable outsider artistic and community organizer Bill Lee, a resident of Fifth Ward, became a mentor to him. Growing up, Purple Bastard was besieged by a myriad of musical styles. At home, he was captivated by soul and classic rock sounds enjoyed by his mother. On the school playground and in his neighborhood, however, hip hop reigned supreme.

Purple Bastard's earliest hip hop influences were an eclectic assortment reflecting both geographic and stylistic diversity. When he was a teen, during the late 1990s and early 2000s, his listening preferences included artists such as Cleveland's Bone Thugs N Harmony, Goodie Mob and OutKast from Atlanta, and New York's Wu-Tang Clan, those being artists who dominated commercial radio during that period. Purple Bastard was especially enamored with the music produced by New Orleans's Mannie Fresh and Virginia's Timbaland, both having idiosyncratic production styles that made major waves in hip hop and R&B during that time. He also enjoyed the work of DJ Screw, which he calls "weird, trippy stuff." All the aforementioned artists were major influences on him as he turned from fan to deejay to producer while attending college at the University of Texas and later the University of Houston in the middle of the first decade of the 2000s.

Purple Bastard describes his music to me as "psychedelic hip-hop homegrown in Houston, Texas." He strongly identifies with the psychedelic label, feeling that it places him within a continuum of artists that dates back to the 1960s. Psychedelic is not an official market genre but a stylistic label, used to describe the music of 1960s countercultural artists such as Jefferson Airplane and the Grateful Dead. These artists created ambient and absorbing sonic bodies, meant for mental, rather than physical, stimulation. According to Craig Morrison (2000), the music was produced to mimic aurally the cognitive effect of the drug LSD, which was popular among counterculturalists. Purple Bastard's style is well within that legacy. Regarding his sound, he tells me, "I like to make my music very psychedelic and engaging—kinda create a sonic atmosphere with what I'm doing. I guess that's the main delineation between psychedelic music and regular music. It's more concerned with the use of space than necessarily all the traditional musical elements. It's concerned with creating an atmosphere or vibe, and it's not just focused on being melodic or stuff like that" (interview with the author, April 2012). Keeping with hip hop convention, Purple Bastard's beats are polyrhythmic and bass heavy. He employs melodies in a traditional way, but accentuates them with a variety of unconventional sounds and often uses vocal samples in a percussive manner. While there are differences between his collaborative and solo instrumental work, his style largely exhibits an aerial density that is in accordance with the psychedelic legacy.

The influence of translocal hip hop and exo–hip hop traditions on Purple Bastard's sound is undeniable. Houston hip hop music and identity, however, is a foundational constituent of his creative expression. The *purple* in That Purple Bastard's name is a nod to Houston's hip hop identity. Musically, the connection between his idiosyncratic style and local aesthetics is even deeper. "Screw is a major influence," he says. In the following, he further elucidates screw's impact on his music: "In my music, I do down-tempo kind of stuff. I do the Screw samples too, just like everybody else does—ya know, slowing down samples, having lower BPMs. You know what I mean. Just as a starting point for music" (interview with the author, April 2012).

Screw music gives Purple Bastard's productions its psychedelic base: "It's psychedelic music, but people on the block fuck with it," he says (interview with the author, April 2012). For him, the screw sound acts as the psychedelic pivot point in his blending of an acutely broad miscellany of styles. Furthermore, he attributes the down-tempo, lo-fi, and bluesiness of his music to the influence of screwtapes. Despite a wide range of influences, he has a deep appreciation for screw, and it is a strong influence on his unique sound.

The Mighty D-Risha was raised on the North East side of Houston, off Freeway 610 and North Wayside Streets, by his grandparents after his parents divorced when he was eight years old. Unlike most Houston hip hoppers, he was educated in private schools, attending St. Francis of Assisi Middle School and graduating from St. Pius High School. He began rapping while in high school. At first, he would freestyle, offering extemporaneous rap performances in the hallways between class periods, in the cafeteria at lunchtime, and at house parties. Later, as he told me, the Northside Houston duo Paul Wall and Chamillionaire influenced him to write his rhymes down: "I was heavily influenced in high school by Paul Wall and Chamillionaire, because ya know, I'm from the Northside. My favorite album is Lil Keke's *Don't Mess with Texas*. But Paul Wall and Chamillionaire's lyricism pushed me to write. Because my friends were like 'they doin' this, they doin' that,' so I was like 'I gotta step my shit up.' So I had to transition from the freestyle rap to having to write everything down" (interview with the author, November 2011). In Paul Wall and Chamillionaire, D-Risha saw a duo of local emcees rapping about the social life in his 'hood, but in a highly lyrical manner, which diverged from that of their contemporaries. While Paul Wall and Chamillionaire influenced him to write, listening to Detroit's Royce the 5'9 taught him how to structure verses and songs: "There was this Royce the 5'9 song with Eminem. I listened to the whole song, and that's how I learned to structure my first 16. Ya know what I'm sayin'. So, just learning from high-quality lyricists and trying to figure out how they did stuff and trying to put it to what I was doing" (interview with the author, November 2011). D-Risha learned the craft of hip hop songwriting by listening to Royce the 5'9, a Detroit artist and longtime collaborator with popular mainstream rapper Eminem. D-Risha also mentions Memphis's Eightball & MJG, Three 6 Mafia Memphis, and New Orleans Mystikal, as well as New York's KRS-One and Jay-Z as early influences. After attending college for two years at the University of Houston-Downtown, he dropped out to pursue music full-time and released his debut album, *The Last Dragon*, in 2009.

D-Risha's diverse experiences and hip hop influences are reflected in his sophomore album, *Big Trouble in Houston, Texas* (2011). On the album, D-Risha negotiates individual agency and allegiance to local hip hop tradition. The album's theme, as reflected in the title, is derived from director John Carpenter's martial arts comedy *Big Trouble in Little China* (1986), one of his favorite films. Musically, the album is grounded in updated boom-bap production, over which D-Risha drops up-tempo verses using his booming,

Figure 10. The Mighty D-Risha. Photo by author.

southern-fried verse. Lyrically, he vacillates between boasts and confessional tales, with a few horror-movie and video game references mixed in for effect. His personal sound is most straightforwardly showcased in "Shake the Heavens," which features fellow local emcees HashBrown and Bishop Black. The song's beat, constructed by Michigan beat maker Apollo Brown, features Wu-Tang Clan–esque[4] horns laid over a James Brown–type "Funky Drummer" drum break. Over the beat, D-Risha aggressively tears through beat with a series of highly lyrical boasts:

> One of the best flows in the city
> Put on the best show are you kidding
> Like a busted condom, you ain't fuckin with me
> Get to duckin' quickly

Fellow local underground rappers HashBrown and Bishop Black follow suit as the three record a song that could have come out of New York a decade before. On "Choices," D-Risha displays an emotional vulnerability not common to the screw tradition and raps about familial discontent over a horn-laden, Apollo Brown beat. "Rampage" features him performing aggressive battle-style verses over the Beastie Boys' "So What'Cha Want" (1992). His *Big*

Trouble in Houston, Texas breaks sharply from Houston hip hop tradition by incorporating a diverse range of sounds and vocal styles.

While grounded in multiregional lyricism and production styles, the music at several moments reflects a strong Houston hip hop influence. "We Holdin" is inspired by slab culture. The term *holdin* is short for "holdin' slab," having a slab vehicle and other markers of street wealth. However, in this context, *holdin* means "holding on," persevering through trials and tribulations as they come. The beat, ironically constructed by Chicago producer Lokey, uses the iconic UGK track "Diamonds and Wood" (1996) as its base, even including the skit that opens the original. D-Risha slows down his vocals to "wax poetic" about the jealousy and envy he faces in Houston's hip hop scene, while guest rapper Herney the Great uses his youthful Southern drawl to discuss issues currently affecting his life.

"Ebonics" is the most direct and explicit reference to Houston hip hop scene identity on *Big Trouble in Houston Texas*. The track, a remix of New York rapper Big L's song of the same name, is a primer on Houston area street slang. D-Risha, in the following lines, informs listeners about the meaning of local colloquialisms, such as *plex*, *fed*, *live*, *tyne*, and *dyne*:

> See when something goes on, it means it goes "live"
> Or you can say it goes "fed" it all depends on your style
> Over there you say town, over here we say "tyne"
> And if it's about to happen then "Mayne its goin' dyne"

In this selection, D-Risha explains local street slang such as *fed* and *live*, words used to describe spectacular or enjoyable activities and events. *Tyne* and *dyne* are dialectical spellings of *town* and *down*, respectively. D-Risha's "Ebonics" is an introduction to the vernacular language of Black working-class Houston, a communicative system that outsiders would find difficult to discern.

On *6 Demon Bag* (2012), their collaborative EP, D-Risha and producer That Purple Bastard remixed "Ebonics" in what D-Risha calls "the most obvious way," by citing Houston's hip hop canon. A canon can be "the repertories and forms of musical behavior constantly shaped by a community to express its cultural particularity and the characteristics that distinguish it as a social entity" (Bohlman 1988, 104). In the Houston hip hop context, D-Risha is talking about the bodies of works that are socially and historically important and function to express the collective identity of this particular social formation. "Ebonics (H-Town Platinum Edition Remix)" contains a mash-up of iconic Houston tracks, including "Tops Drop" by Fat Pat, "Back Back" by Lil O, and "Mind Playin' Tricks" by the Geto Boys. The presence of the Houston hip hop canon illuminates D-Risha's ownership of Houston hip hop identity. At the same time, however, he maintains his underground identity through unorthodox elements, such as the reverb on his vocals. Therefore, on the "Ebonics" remix, we again witness the fusion of personal and communal musical identities.

D-Risha and That Purple Bastard make explicit local references throughout the 6 Demon Bag EP. "We Hold / So Cold (Grey Tape Remix)," Purple Bastard's remix to "We Holdin," sonically recalls the feel of an original screwtape, as suggested by the suffix. He replaces Lokey's original track with a slower instrumental built off of a sample of R&B artist Keith Sweat's 1985 song "Make It Last Forever," the same sample used on the Screwed Up Click's (Botany Boyz, E.S.G., Big Moe) popular song "Making Cash Forever" (1998). The requisite chops and cuts that defined DJ Screw's turntable performance are interspersed throughout the track. Purple Bastard even lowered the song's fidelity to reflect accurately the analog, cassette-based sound of original DJ Screw tapes.

D-Risha's music reflects a strong East Coast hip hop influence, with sporadic overtures to local hip hop identity. These references to locality, D-Risha said to me, are strategic measures that enable him to gain the attention of otherwise uninterested local audiences: "Being from Houston, you can't make an East Coast–based project. It's not gonna go over well. I kind have to give them that pill [screw] so they can take in my other concepts. That's why I do songs like 'Ebonics'" (interview with the author, November 2011). Houston audiences, by and large, have little value for D-Risha's eclectic version of hip hop music. Therefore, he offers them "pills," locally identified songs like "Ebonics," as well as "We Holdin" and "Nightrider," that establish sonic relevance and show that he has a firm commitment to local tradition and identity. These intermittent references to Houston hip hop tradition allow him to create a space for himself, albeit a small one, in Houston's rap scene.

Similar to D-Risha, Nasty Nique Roots's dualistic musical identity reflects his dynamic social background. As a member of the group Dirty & Nasty, he produces mainstream-oriented music that occasionally reflects a Houston hip hop identity. However, as a solo artist, he makes avant-garde rap that draws upon cross-cultural markers of local identity, such as Houston's professional sports team and retail outlets. In short, whereas his group work is firmly situated within Houston's hip hop aesthetic, his solo work is experimental.

Nasty Nique's complex musical identity is informed by dynamic personal history and musical influences. He was born Tomanique Roots in Chicago, Illinois, and lived briefly in Atlanta, Georgia, and Hartford, Connecticut, before settling in Southwest Houston during his adolescence. Nasty Nique spent his freshman year of high school at Westbury High School. In fact, we were there at the same time, though we did not cross paths. It was at Westbury where he first engaged with hip hop culture. Unlike most Houston rap artists who cite music as their first encounter with hip hop, Nique got into hip hop through graffiti art, which he used to protest the poor conditions at the school: "Westbury had just gotten some allotment from HISD [Houston Independent School District], but they chose to spend the money on the offices and all that first. But we had leaks in the gym.... You know, it was like ... this is bullshit. So, I was like, 'Fuck it. I'ma write on it and redecorate it'" (interview with the author, November 2011).

From there, Nasty Nique immersed himself in hip hop. He built his cultural knowledge and honed his skills while attending the predominantly Hispanic Milby High School on the Southeast side, to which he transferred after his ninth-grade year. Nique, who is African American, told me that his time at Milby was a "culture shock," which forced him to "reexamine his culture and ideas of community." While jarring, Milby facilitated his growth in hip hop culture. He moved from graffiti to b-boying and later to deejaying after meeting classmate DJ Arsanik Gomez, who owned a pair of turntables. He eventually settled on emceeing after seeing a video by rapper Nas on the cable network BET (Black Entertainment Television). He says, "I saw the 'Nas Is Like' video. I saw it on MTV and was like, 'I can do that.'" After graduating from Milby High School, Nique matriculated to Houston's University of St. Thomas, earning a degree in business.

Nasty Nique Roots's solo work is largely experimental or avant-garde. He employs a wide variety of themes and styles, most of which are foreign to Houston's screw tradition. "Westbury Get the Money," a song from his 2011 EP *Breakfast of Champions*, is a good representation of his style. "Westbury Get the Money," a remake of rapper Nas's "Queens Get the Money" (2009), is an ode to the Southwest Houston community. He borrows the beat for the song from OutKast's "E.T.: Extraterrestrial," produced by members Andre 3000 and Big Boi. Like its predecessor, the beat lacks drums and has little

Figure 11. Nasty Nique Roots. Photo by author.

bass, two core features of Houston's local sound. Furthermore, Nasty Nique Roots's stream-of-consciousness flow breaks from local conventions: loosely structured, it includes rapid shifts from topic to topic and examples of cryptic language. He uses this unorthodox style to convey a snapshot of typical youth experience in Westbury:

> Yep Idea was Westbury's Nike vandal, the kid with the Marbury handles
> The same kid who use to come to school in them Payless sandals
> Took on that graffiti handle to give niggas ideas that they could not handle
> And proceeded to knock 'em out the park like Mickey Mantle

"Westbury Get Money" is a coming-of-age story about Nasty Nique's life on the Southwest side of Houston. He opens with discussion of his high-school days, which appears to be a transitional phase for him. Shoes act as a metaphor for this transition. Earlier in his life, he used to wear Payless sandals, from a shoe company known for selling inexpensive, low-end products. At his high school, high-end, name-brand clothing was among the highest forms of cultural capital, and wearing Payless sandals could render a student unpopular. However, that was not his high school experience. He wore Nike shoes and was a talented basketball player; hence, "Yep Idea was Westbury's Nike vandal, the kid with the Marbury handles" (*Idea* was Nasty Nique's graffiti tag, and Stephon Marbury was a professional basketball player known for his ability to dribble a basket-ball). He details stealing cigarillos from Randall's, a popular Houston-based grocery store, and then using them to smoke marijuana in nearby Hagar Park. The story, in its totality, is unique to Southwest Houston. While references to Westbury and Hagar Park reflect this geographic exactness, the icons of high-status teen life and familiar tales of youthful mischievousness are relatable to a wide base of Houstonians. That is, the social importance of clothing, shoplift-ing, and the use of recreational drugs are elements relatable to a cross section of Houston young adults from both inner-city and suburban backgrounds. "Westbury Get Money" is not a tale of the streets: rather, it is a story of raucous youth indiscretion, grounded geographically in urban Houston.

Breakfast of Champions is a concept album, centered on the Houston Rock-ets basketball team's back-to-back National Basketball Association champi-onships in 1994 and 1995. A concept album is a studio album that features a single theme or idea. While concept albums are uncommon within the dominant Houston hip hop scene, they are popular among underground hip hop emcees because they test an artist's creativity and are markers of superior skill. Nasty Nique's use of a concept is less self-centered and rooted in civic pride. He explained:

> I just remember back to that time man, that time period, being an ele-mentary-aged kid when the Rockets were winning and were champions. Ya know, that two-and-a-half-year span when they were on top of the basketball world. Everybody in the city was just buzzing and on fire. The city just had a confidence. It was just like, you could talk to strangers on the bus and be like "how about that Rocket game?" ... So I wanted to take people back and, like, kind of remind people, ya know, like when we were champions, when we were on top. That same confidence and that same spirit. Man, the city's lost it. (Interview with the author, November 2011)

His commentary invokes the Houston Rockets' championship seasons to remind Houstonians of the competitive fire and confidence that once per-meated the city. Nasty Nique Roots seeks to restore pride across Houston by using the Houston Rockets' championship as a concept. His target audience is not the streets, nor the hip hop scene exclusively, but the many communi-ties that make up the city of Houston. On *Breakfast of Champions*, he uses iconic markers to express inclusivity, to express a civic pride rooted in the multicultural local experience, rather than the particularities of the street.

Personal tastes are the strongest influence on Nasty Nique Roots's solo records: "I put out these records because it's stuff I want to hear," he told me. "It's stuff that I think is dope." He calls these solo projects "blog-type" releases because their experimental styles are popular on blogs such as Steadybloggin .com, which has featured him many times. While receiving blog attention, these projects—characterized by avant-garde vocal performances, abstruse lyricism, and creative concepts—are not popular among the screw fans who dominate the local scene. These records exhibit strong local identity, as exhibited in his neighborhood anthems and local sports themes, but are stylistically too far left of the screw center to catch the attention of most local hip hop fans.

Nasty Nique makes overtures toward Houston's core hip hop audience as a member of Dirty & Nasty, along with rapper Dirty Dog D. The duo, formed in 2007, eschews the inventiveness of Nasty Nique's solo work in favor of a sound that reflects popular local musical trends. "With Dirty & Nasty, we make songs that are beat- and melody-oriented," he says. "These are songs that I could hear on the radio." Their *Fools Gold* EP, released in February 2012, is a diverse album in terms of production and lyrical content. The track "All Black Everything," for example, is a danceable exploration of modern society using Black Power as a frame of reference. On "Kiss The Sky," Nasty Nique, D3, and guest Kyle Hubbard turn introspective, conveying the fluid emotions attached to ambition. "Sex in the Beat" is a smooth dedication to the opposite sex.

Dirty & Nasty show their allegiance to and reverence for local hip hop tradition on "Parking Lot Pimpin' Remix," *Fools Gold*'s most popular song and one that has become a staple of their live shows. It is firmly rooted in the Houston sound. The beat, produced by Big Boy Tracks, is a screw-based production that features the "rollin' drum pattern," heavy synthesizers, and scattered organ sounds. The chorus features "screwed" vocal lines from Pimp C, Mike Jones, and Bun B, all in reference to Houston's slab culture. Lyrically, Nasty Nique's verse is in accordance with the established Houston aesthetic:

> They got the parking lot looking like a freak show
> I got a couple cups, poured up ice cold
> Got a couple cups, doubled up Carmelo
> I see a couple girls' fine ass yellow bones

Nasty Nique's verse includes several markers of Houston identity. "Double cups" is a reference to Houston's lean or syrup culture. "Fine ass yellow bone" refers to African American women with light complexions. During the 1990s, members of the Screwed Up Click and other cultural participants frequently referenced such women in lyrics, as they were notable status symbols. Later in the song, Nasty Nique mentions "Showin' naked ass," a phrase popularized by Screwed Up Click member Lil Keke that means to boldly seize attention or make your presence felt. This phrase has become a popular idiom within Houston hip hop culture. Finally, Nasty Nique reps his 'hood, the Southwest (of the Astrodome), exhibiting a core component of local hip hop tradition.

To further cement their Houston hip hop identity, Dirty & Nasty released *Chopped Gold* (2012), a "chopped not slopped" version of their *Fools Gold* EP, remixed by OG Ron C. "Chopped not slopped" is OG Ron C's take on the screwed-and-chopped style developed by DJ Screw. In the wake of DJ Screw's death, OG Ron C and Michael Watts have become key purveyors of the tradition. Many artists, both inside and outside of Houston, employ OG Ron C to place a Houston stamp of their music. His remix of *Fools Gold*, renamed *Chopped Gold*, reinforces Dirty & Nasty's cultural identity.

Making Space Through Live Performance

Underground hip hop artists reflect diverse experiences and employ styles that move them away from the screw tradition and toward the periphery of the scene, existing in relative obscurity. Whereas street artists can sell records and get radio play and are often covered in both hip hop–related and mainstream media, underground artists are declined access to the local hip hop infrastructure. As a result, they have to create space for themselves within the Houston hip hop scene. They must find ways to expose themselves and their music to a base of listeners who would be open to their style of hip hop. Live performance is the primary way that they negotiate space within Houston's screw-dominated hip hop scene.

Live performances are vital to the sustenance of any music scene, but underground artists in Houston do not give many live shows. This is not for lack of space, as Houston has a plethora of live music venues: "Warehouse Live, House of Blues, Fitzgerald's, Last Concert Café, Sambuca, Concert Pub, Danelectro's, Firehouse Saloon and The Hideaway are just a handful of the many venues that offer live local music in the Houston area" (Waites 2012). This large collective of venues, however, is resistant to booking hip hop shows, especially when it comes to underground artists. As D-Risha notes, "That's the central thing: money. What they do makes a lot of easy money. What we do is kind of like a grind thing. We gotta scrape up; we gotta race to the finish line. They just don't get what we're doin', and they don't really respect it. So it doesn't last long. They being venues and club promoters. Mainly venues, they're not opening arms to hip hop shows" (interview with the author, November 2011). Underground artists in Houston do not have dedicated audiences. Plus, the audience that they do have is rarely willing to pay the price of admission. As a result, venues in Houston are less willing to book hip hop shows that cannot guarantee profitable returns.

When given performance opportunities, underground artists are often forced to undertake measures that ensure the economic viability of their appearances. They often pay to perform as the opening acts for popular national artists—a practice commonly called "pay for play." Recognizing the relative value of a performance slot next to a major artist, concert promoters can charge up-and-coming artists looking for exposure. This system proves to be a financial windfall for promoters because they receive money for artists who would otherwise be paid, while earning money off ticket purchases.

In the following commentary, D-Risha discusses how popular concert promoter Scoremore uses a practice called "the showdown" to select opening acts for popular artists:

> I would love to get on those big shows, but that's a lot harder to do. A lot of pay-for-play bullshit goin' on there. Aw man, say no to pay for play! Basically, it's like selling tickets and getting no residuals. Scoremore is bringing all these big cats. They have a system called ... It's a Showdown. OK, me and you are artists, right? Me and you are competing to be the opener. That's some bullshit. If I sell more tickets than you, then I get to open up. That's bullshit, that's pay for play. Say no to pay for play, dawg! (Interview with the author, November 2011)

Austin, Texas–based Scoremore, which became a subsidiary of concert promotion company Live Nation in 2018, is one of the more prolific promotional teams operating in the Houston area. By determining opening-act slots based on ticket sales, it more than ensures a profitable return on the slot while securing extra promotional vehicles for its shows.

Scoremore and other promoters recognize that opening-act slots are of prime importance to underground artists. Opening for mid-level or mainstream acts allows underground artists to perform to larger crowds, building their audience and raising their profile within the scene. The use of opening acts, at least within the Houston hip hop scene, appears to be a method used by promoters to maximize profits. In general, headlining artists' sets are typically no longer than an hour. Paying audiences, however, expect much more than an hour of music. Therefore, a hip hop show commonly has two to four opening acts, playing for one to two hours before the headliner's set. During this time, the venue earns money from the bar.

Given the difficulty of finding performance opportunities within the hip hop scene, underground artists commonly perform before nontraditional hip hop audiences. For example, on November 19, 2011, D-Risha and Bishop Black performed at Twenty Below Sports Bar in Katy, Texas, a populous working- to middle-class suburb north of Houston. DJ Craig Reap, an underground deejay, is a Katy native and has sought to cultivate hip hop there. The show's audience reflected Twenty Below Sports Bar's typical patronage: White men and women in their thirties and forties. As an African American male in his late twenties, I stood out from the crowd to such an extent that DJ Craig Reap, sensing that I was somehow connected to the local hip hop scene, introduced himself to me. During the show, I sat next to a group of middle-aged White men, who, with their handkerchief-covered heads and badge-covered jackets, appeared to belong to a motorcycle club. Their strong lack of interest in the musical performances reflected the general attitude of the audience. D-Risha and Bishop Black offered dynamic sets but could not capture the crowd, which likely felt that the hip hop show interfered with their normal Monday night. Such receptions are not uncommon for underground artists as they seek to disseminate their music whenever given the opportunity.

When local underground artists open for larger acts, they use the opportunity to introduce themselves, their crews, and the general underground hip hop sector to audience members. D-Risha's February 18, 2012, show at Numbers Nightclub is a good example of this practice. D-Risha opened for Mike Relm, a San Francisco–based deejay/veejay, who has an innovative show centered on his use of turntables to manipulate music videos. Numbers Nightclub is one of the oldest live music venues in Houston, nestled in the heart of the city's eclectic Montrose neighborhood. It is a traditionally indie rock–oriented space, but features deejays spinning EDM, house, and techno several nights a week. Mike Relm's show was one of its rare hip hop–related events.

For D-Risha, the Mike Relm show was a particularly good opportunity because it would bring out the scattered base of hip hop fans whose listening practices move beyond the limits of screw. Mike Relm is a descendent of the San Francisco turntabilism movement that emerged in the mid-1990s. Turntabilism involves using turntables and mixers to manipulate recordings in the creation of a new musical product. While screwed-and-chopped music could be considered a branch of turntabilism, the genre is not popular among Houston's screw audience. That night's crew was likely composed of people whose musical tastes are not centered on screw. They would be more receptive to his style of hip hop than would traditional Houston hip hop audiences.

I arrived at Numbers around 9:00 p.m., an hour after doors opened. I quickly realized that I was still early. The venue's staff was preparing the stage, and I was one of fewer than ten people in the audience. By 11:00 p.m., the crowd had grown slightly, up to approximately fifty people, but far less than the capacity of the venue. That Purple Bastard, whom I bumped into before D-Risha's set, attributed the poor attendance to bad weather. It had rained heavily earlier in the day. Nevertheless, Purple Bastard was not the only rap artist in the crowd at that point. I recognized several rappers whom I had seen perform during my time in the field. Since this was an all-ages show, there was a fairly wide age range among the audience. The majority of attendees appeared to be between 18 and 22 years old, but a significant number of attendees appeared to be outside of that age group. The crowd was overwhelmingly White, with Hispanics running a distant second. It was difficult to distinguish rappers from audience members among the African Americans in attendance, but I noticed around four, other than myself, who did not appear to be affiliated with rap artists. Similar to the other rap performances I had attended during my research period, the audience was around 70 percent male, and most of the women in attendance appeared to be with male companions.

The racial composition of the Numbers audience is not unusual for D-Risha; his audiences are usually majority White. He speculates that these White fans are, in reality, indie rock audiences who become exposed to his music when he plays rock-oriented venues like Numbers. Nevertheless, they express a strong interest in his music, as he notes: "The rock crowd is more accepting of what we do. Whenever I have my live show, they get into it. Not just me, but they're more accepting to it. They want to know where they can buy my CD. If I have merch, they're more asking, 'Hey, hey, hey.' They're more fans" (interview with the author, November 2012).

Rock audiences may be attracted to D-Risha's live performances because they often have a rock feel to them. This is especially true when he performs with drummer Sir Mikol, as he did that night. Sir Mikol, an important figure in Houston's funk and rock scenes, gives D-Risha's shows punk rock and nu-metal sensibilities. By contrast, according to D-Risha, Black audiences have shown little interest in his music. "Black crowds ain't tryin' to hear shit I'm sayin,'" he jokes. He suspects that their lack of interest is fueled by his nonlocally identified style.

After an introduction by host B-Boy Craig, D-Risha, accompanied by Dirty & Nasty, Misfit Crazy Eight, and Purple Bastard, entered a stage already flanked by DJ Arsanik to the far right and drummer Sir Mikol at the center. D-Risha, D3, and Nasty Nique Roots wore D-Risha T-shirts, while DJ Arsanik wore a shirt that read "Space City Beat Battle" across the front. After warming up the crowd for a minute or two, D-Risha dove into his first song, "Save the Day" remix, with Dirty & Nasty serving as hypemen.[5] "Save the Day" and the following song, "Rampage," were performed with breathless intensity. The RSA crew were having fun, with perpetual smiles on their faces.

After "Rampage," in a show of crew solidarity, D-Risha allowed Dirty & Nasty to take the stage; they performed two of their signature songs, "Rick Flair Swagger" and "Parking Lot Pimping." This was a generous move on D-Risha's part. The spotlight is always fleeting for underground artists. He empowered Dirty & Nasty by allowing them to perform during his set, but doing so further condensed his already slight moment of exposure. Such measures reflect the Rogue Scholars Alliance's core principals. "We come together for a common purpose," D-Risha once told me. "We come together to support each other."

TURNIN' HEADZ SHOWCASE: REDEFINING THE BOUNDARIES OF THE HOUSTON HIP HOP SCENE

Although Houston's underground artists can further their careers by sharing the bill with larger, non–Houston-based hip hop acts, they understand that local success depends on establishing a secure fan base within the city.

They must cultivate an audience that is willing to purchase their materials consistently, attend their shows, and further the discourse about them. It is difficult for underground artists. They do not have a consistent media presence, and their live performances are infrequent. Furthermore, the world of popular music trends is defined by limited attention spans. If one is away from the limelight for too long, even the most dedicated fans will turn their gaze elsewhere.

It is for this reason that underground artists have created venues through which they can build their community. One such venue is the Turnin' Headz Showcase, a monthly hip hop event established in 2011. Occurring on the first Thursday evening of every month, it brings local hip hoppers together to fellowship within the context of performance. Every week, it allows local emcees to present their skills in front of an attentive and receptive audience. It has changed its location several times, and I attended the shows thrown at Check Other Outfitters.

The Turnin' Headz showcase is not a novel idea in the hip hop landscape. Underground hip hop artists across the country have developed spaces that allow them to present their crafts in the face of mainstream hip hop hegemony. The Los Angeles–based Good Life Café, in the mid-1990s, was arguably the most prominent, locally specific underground hip hop community. The Los Angeles hip hop scene was then being dominated by the gangsta-rap sounds of artists such as Dr. Dre and MC Eiht, making it difficult for non-gangsta artists to achieve local relevance. While the Good Life was open to all styles, the rules—the bans on cursing and gimmicks in particular—made it a particularly functional space for lyrically dynamic artists to shine. The Good Life Café, and its later manifestation, Project Blowed, created an underground movement that allowed non-gangsta LA artists such as Aceyalone, Abstract Rude, and Busdriver to have productive commercial careers (Morgan 2009).

Although organized by a collective that actively identifies with the underground hip hop label, Turnin' Headz: Blank Canvas is a musically diverse talent showcase, and the lineup for the May 3, 2012, showcase bears witness to this. The show's opener, J-Mak the Monsta, performed wearing a generic yellow polo shirt and jeans, eschewing popular hip hop fashion trends. He resembled a "hip hop everyman," and his performance, characterized by a focus on clean but battle-oriented lyrics, delivered in a straightforward way, followed suit. Conversely, Smashsation, who followed J-Mak, is a Galveston-raised emcee whose pimp rap–infused style is reminiscent of Texas legend Pimp C. Closing out the night was Doublebe, part of the Headwreckas crew with Doughbeezy. Doublebe is a native of Houston but spent significant time in Atlanta, and his style reflects both influences. His performance was grounded in Houston-based lyricism and tone, but his delivery and production were reminiscent of Atlanta artists such as T.I. and Young Jeezy.

The diversity in Turnin' Headz: Blank Canvas represents Purple Bastard's and other underground artists' attempt to reshape the boundaries of the Houston hip hop scene. They seek to expand the definition of what it means to be a Houston hip hop artist. Purple Bastard told me, "I always made it a point to book a bunch of different kinds of acts together. You know what I mean? I would book those old heads, you know, but I would book them on a show with somebody who was more "hood.' You know what I mean? And somebody who was totally experimental. You know what I mean? And have those three elements come together or have those seemingly incompatible elements come together on the same show or same stage and just make good music" (interview with the author, 2012).

The variety of acts within the makeup of Turnin' Headz reflects the founder's desire to create "a scene as richly diverse as the artists that made it up."

The underground understanding of "scene," as exemplified through Turnin' Headz, is grounded much more in community than in principle. While recognizing the value in core aesthetics, they view the local scene more as a community composed of participants with disparate styles whose contributions should be of equal value. For them, it would be a scene where the abstract style of Nasty Nique Roots can coexist alongside the Houston traditionalism of E.S.G., and Purple Bastard's syrupy, psychedelic productions would be recognized as a legitimate descendent of DJ Screw as opposed to a bastard child. To accomplish this, they continue to push boundaries, make spaces, and build relationships with the hope that these efforts will one day translate into a stylistic diversity within the hip hop scene that reflects the ethnic diversity within the city.

6

ONE CITY UNDER GOD

Blessings Christian Bookstore occupies the rightmost corner of a small yellow multiunit building on Homestead Road on the north side of Houston. Its neighbors are a small, inconspicuous church and, oddly, a flower shop, which takes visual prominence among the tenants because of a large sign that hangs above its door. Blessings's proprietor, Andre Barnes, is a tall, hulking African American man, whose dominating appearance is softened by the giant smile that lights up his face as he greets you. Any perceived physical intimidation is further dismissed when he opens his mouth and reveals a velvety smooth voice. He sits at a small desk at the back of the store, where he watches over the shelves that hold his inventory and keeps a keen eye on everyone who walks through the door.

I visited Blessings on an August evening to talk with Andre Barnes about Christian hip hop, a topic with which he has intimate knowledge. For the last several years, he has recorded Christian hip hop music in Houston under the name 007 (pronounced Double-Oh-Seven). The Houston-based Much Luvv Records released his debut album, *Audio Future* (2010), to much acclaim. He followed this release with *The City Never Sleeps* (2013), a collaboration album with fellow Houston Christian rapper Gifted the Flamethrowa.

Although relatively new to Christian hip hop, 007 is an OG (original gangster) in the secular rap world. He is a member of the legendary Houston rap group the 5th Ward Boyz, who released a string of popular albums for Rap-A-Lot Records throughout the 1990s. The 5th Ward Boyz produced funky yet gritty music that documented Houston's inner-city street life. Their singles and videos, such as "Situations," "Ghetto Funk," and especially "P.W.A.," earned them a strong fan base, in and beyond Houston. They performed all over the world, sharing bills with rap luminaries such as 2pac Shakur and Jay-Z.

Barnes's life changed after he served time for a string of bank robberies that he admits committing in the Houston area. He had turned to crime not out of necessity but out of an existential desire: "I could not separate the streets from the music," he says; the bank robberies made him feel "free" and "invincible." At the time of his arrest, he had a wife and two small children at home. He was sentenced to sixty years in prison in Falfurrias, Texas, geographically and culturally far away from his Houston roots. While imprisoned in 2005, he connected with a spiritual advisor, a local pastor, who taught him a Protestant version of Christian principles. He eventually gave his life to Christ in January of 2006, and his newfound faith was quickly tested when his younger brother died. That death shook his new spiritual foundation. Nevertheless, he remained resilient. While in the prison, he made a deal with God, promising to change his life if he were released: "I made a covenant with God," he says; "if I'm to go home, I will do for my family, I will take my children to church, I will put a spiritual foundation in my life" (interview with the author, 2012).

After being released from prison in 2007, Barnes opened Blessings Christian Bookstore, with money his wife had saved while he was incarcerated. Through the bookstore and his church home, he maintained a solid Christian base. Though Houston had a solid Christian rap community, he no longer had any interest in rap. In fact, he had sworn off rap after his conversion, and he believed that Christian rap was, as he said, "wack." However, after hearing the music of the Houston-based Soldiers on a Mission (S.O.M.) and the Dallas-based 116 Clique, he realized the possibilities of Christian rap music, which led to his early recordings at a neighboring studio.

For Barnes, Christian rap is a way that he can connect and proselytize to those in the streets. He says, "My focus is to get dudes on the corner to say 'If he can change, then I can change.'" It is for this reason that his music is firmly grounded in street realities. This ethic holds true for his fellow Houston-based Christian hip hop artists as well, rappers who embrace secular Houston hip hop heritage, rather than distancing themselves from it. These artists engage with secular hip hop content as a way to gain respect in the streets, in the local hip hop scene, and in sacred spaces around the city. Christian hip hop artists are positioned at the nexus of these three spaces. Their spiritual ideals are developed in sacred space, as is their core audience, but their ministerial efforts are focused on bringing street actors out of street space. Local hip hop heritage becomes a way to communicate with the streets. Christian artists must carefully and strategically navigate these three spaces in their sacred-secular fusion.

CHRISTIAN HIP HOP: ENTERTAINMENT AND MINISTRY

Similar to underground hip hop artists, Christian hip hop artists operate along the margins of the Houston hip hop scene. They primarily perform music within the confines of the church, rather than at block parties, clubs, bars, and clothing stores. Life Radio, an hour-long radio program that is broadcast Wednesday nights on Houston's public radio station KPFT, is one of a few radio programs, terrestrial or virtual, that disseminate the music. Sketch the Journalist, a longtime local Christian hip hop fan and collector, almost single-handedly manages media coverage for the community. While somewhat isolated, Houston's Christian hip hop community has produced a number of artists who have achieved national success, including Lil Raskull, Von Won, Tre-9, Corey Paul, and Andre "007" Barnes.

Christian hip hop music in Houston has dual functions, simultaneously operating as entertainment and ministry. The function of the music shifts to match its audience. "For people that's saved already, this is your entertainment," says 007, "but for people that need a Word[1] out of this, and rap is all they listen to, this is ministry for them" (interview with the author, July 2012). Sandra L. Barnes (no relation), in a study of the use of Christian hip hop in predominantly African American churches, says that Christian rappers use the medium "to evangelize to young audiences who are interested in both Christianity and the hip hop culture" (2008, 324). Christian rap enables the saved to enjoy one of the most popular contemporary music styles without simultaneously consuming content that compromises their Christian principles. It is "sanctified entertainment," to borrow a phrase from John Styll, editor of *Contemporary Christian Music*, a monthly online magazine. It is music that "has all the diversionary value of entertainment, but ... is infused with the power of the Gospel" (Styll 1986, 4). "Christians like to groove, too," as Andre Barnes notes, and Christian hip hop enables them to do so within the framework of their spiritual worldview.

The concept of ministry undergirds Houston-based Christian rappers' approach to music making. Ministry, at its most fundamental level, refers to the Christian practice of communicating God's word. In *Apostles of Rock: The Splintered World of Contemporary Christian Music*, an exploration of the social and economic dynamics of contemporary Christian music, Jay R. Howard and John M. Streck offer a contemporary evangelical definition of ministry: "The concept of ministry comprises three identifiably distinct but intertwined objectives: evangelism—the effort to convince the non-Christian to affirm the fundamental tenets of the Christian faith and to 'accept Jesus Christ as his or her personal savior'; worship facilitation—the attempt to allow God to manifest himself in the presence of believers or to allow believers to communicate with Him; and exhortation—the encouragement of the believer in his or her 'Christian walk'" (1999, 54).

Of these three tenets of ministry, evangelism is the key to Christian hip hop's mission. Rappers see their music as a conduit of Christian belief in the secular world. They focus on the streets, which they see as a site of spiritual struggle. Garth Kasimu Baker-Fletcher in his article "African American Christian Rap: Facing 'Truth' and Resisting It," suggests that "Christian rap sets about its tasks of proclaiming the saving message (or 'Gospel') of Jesus Christ within the space inhabited by 'homies' who live in 'da world' on 'da streetz'" (2003, 30). In their worldview, street-related behaviors such as drug dealing, prostitution, and interpersonal violence reflect a state of spiritual displacement. The world is a modern-day Sodom and Gomorrah, where, instead of the Christian God, sex, money, and drugs rule. In the song "Choose," 007 explicitly communicates this perspective, telling street occupants they must "choose, on this day, whom you'll serve." He uses this creative reference to the biblical scripture Joshua 24:15 to suggest the incompatibility of serving God and idolizing wealth or other "worldly" activities. Christian rappers warn those in the 'hood against the perils of the streets and implore street occupants to change their lives by placing God at the center. Barnes and others take on the task of bringing the streets to Christ, saving them from experiencing the fate of Sodom and Gomorrah and other signs of a spiritual disconnectedness.

Christian hip hop artists use music as a tool to communicate the message of Christ in the streets. Christian hip hop is ministry in action. Rather than waiting for individuals to "come to the church," the music brings the church to the people. Christian hip hop is a ministry that goes beyond the sacred space of the church. It invades the separate, and at times hesitant, social sphere of the streets. As Barnes told me, it is a response to ministerial practices of traditional Black churches, which have been criticized for not reaching beyond their sacred spaces: "You know, it's like we have this church syndrome. You know, the four walls syndrome. It's like, that's when you feel activated. You know, you dance in there. You can witness in there. But what about the corner?" (interview with the author, July 2012).

Barnes implores his fellow church members to move their evangelizing beyond the sanctuary and take it to the corner, a popular site of economic and social activity within the street. He calls upon congregations to determine how to deliver the message to those in the streets. For him, hip hop music is the answer. Rapper Von Won explains Christian rap's unique effectiveness in ministering to people in the street:

> The rap is just a tool for the ministry. Because I'm a minister, trying to tell people about Jesus, but luckily I got this thing called rap that makes it a lot easier. I think of it like when your mother wanted to give you medicine, you gotta take the medicine, but they smash it up and put it in the orange juice. You know what I'm sayin'. You drink it. It doesn't dilute the medicine. It's all in there, but the orange juice makes it easier to take in. (Interview with the author, July 2012)

Rap music presents the Christian message in a form that resonates with street-based audiences; however, if the message does not embody cultural symbols familiar to the street audience, it can be seen as culturally irrelevant to those who are not actively engaged with Christian church culture. Listeners might feel such spiritual discomfort that they are unable to receive the message. Local Christian hip hop artists' effectiveness as music ministers is determined by their ability to relate to life in the streets. The music must exhibit an intimate understanding of and relationship with street culture. Embracing local secular hip hop styles is particularly effective in this way.

Testimony as Ministerial Method

Conversion (or salvation) testimony, popular in the evangelical tradition, is one of the primary rhetorical approaches that Houston-based Christian rappers employ in their music. Using the oratorical language and style of their religious group, these testimonies are personal narratives that detail the process of one's salvation. They follow a common formula, whereby the narrator begins by describing his or her troublesome life before committing to Christ, moves to the moment of conversion, and closes by illuminating life in the church. In church settings, such testimonies are commonly employed by the saved to consolidate the individual's commitment to the church and reinforce the church community's basic principles and goals.

In Houston's Christian hip hop scene, testimonies are a strategic way of expressing God's power to the unconverted. Rappers "base their lyrics on testimonials which proclaim their former lives before they had a living and personal relationship with Jesus Christ. What is interesting is that they still see themselves as homies, but as homies transformed by the Gospel of Jesus Christ" (Baker-Fletcher 2003, 31). Considering the importance of testimony to Christian rap content, in the following section I present the testimonies of two local Christian hip hop artists, Lil Raskull and Von Won, whose music is strongly informed by street realities and the secular hip hop tradition.

LIL RASKULL

Lil Raskull was born Delbert Harris in Trinity Gardens, the notorious Northside neighborhood that sits adjacent to Fifth Ward. His mother was a single parent who raised him and his two siblings in a poor but stable household. "My mom did good," he told me. "I never missed a meal. It probably wasn't the best meal, but you know" (interview with the author, July 2012). Despite her resolve, she could not shield him from the harsh effects of the 'hood. He recalls living next to a prostitute and frequently witnessing intravenous drug use as a child.

Lil Raskull began selling crack as a teen in the late 1980s. "That's what you did where I grew up," he says. "Everybody had money problems, so the trend was that you move the happy feelings: you move the stuff that makes people feel good." As a crack dealer in one of Houston's roughest areas, Lil

Raskull was not immune to the violence of the street. "I have shot at some people. I can't tell I killed somebody. If I did, I don't know," he says in a joking but sincere manner. Imminent death was very real for Raskull, as many of his friends succumbed to the streets. Many others experienced long-term incarceration, a kind of social death.

Raskull developed a love for hip hop music while living the life of the street. He was first a fan of LL Cool J, whose bravado and voracious rhyme style appealed to him. Later, he took a strong interest in the gangsta sounds of groups like N.W.A. After high school, he began writing raps that documented his and his peers' street activities. He cultivated his skill overtime and eventually signed a recording contract with Dead Game Records, a label owned and operated by a collective of Northside drug dealers. His debut album, *Like a Grown As Man* (1995), was rooted in gangsta-style rap and inspired by his lifestyle. It was well received for its funk-based grooves and Raskull's lyrical depiction of Northside street life. He calls it a Northside classic, one that sold nearly ten thousand units in the Houston area.

Despite his commercial success and increasing fame, Raskull suffered from internal turmoil:

> Something was happening to me supernaturally. Because here I was on the rise with a hit record, people loving it. I was flirting with some major labels to get a deal. But I can't picture a time in life when I was more miserable, man. And I had no idea why. Naturally, I'm just like everybody else. I'm looking at what's going on, and I'm like "It's about to happen." But I can't get this feeling out of me, man. I got invited to church by a friend of mine. And here it is, another supernatural statement. When I walked into the church, a peace just came over me, man. And I never been a dummy, man. I knew it was God. I knew it was God saying, "All right, man. Time's up for what you're doing out there." So I gave it up. (Interview with the author, July 2012)

Lil Raskull believes his conversion to Christianity was the result of supernatural intervention. His time spent either in the streets or rapping about the streets created spiritual turmoil, which was resolved when he fully embraced God. He quit selling drugs and secured a release from his Dead Game contract in order to cultivate his newfound spirituality. Though now a Christian, he initially hesitated to write Christian raps, as he had little knowledge about the scene and market. His mentality changed, however, after a second supernatural intervention:

> On New Year's, a lady came to me, at my church. I think it was New Years of '96. And she began to speak to me about what she believed God was saying to me. And she was rhyming while she was saying it. And she didn't tell me that this is what God wanted me to do, but she was saying, "God wants you to come out of the crowd and come into the clouds." And she was just goin' on and rhyming, man. And when that happened to me, I knew what God was saying to me: "That I want you to pick up the mic again and do it for me." (Interview with the author, July 2012)

Seeking a recording home, Lil Raskull partnered with Knolly Williams, a fellow recently born-again Christian, who had moved to Texas from Los Angeles to escape the streets. Williams formed Grapetree Records to offer a space for former gangsters, like Raskull, who desired to "rap for the Lord." His first Christian release, *Controverse Allstars* (1996), was met with much critical acclaim around Houston. The word *controverse* is a play on the word *controversy* and the famous Chuck Taylor All-Star basketball shoes made by the Converse shoe company. The album's title reflects the daring nature of Raskull's street-tinged Christian music. Since this initial album, Lil Raskull has released more than a dozen solo and group projects and is widely considered a luminary within the Christian rap community, both locally and nationally.

VON WON

Von Won was born Vaughaligan Walwyn in St. Croix, U.S. Virgin Islands. His father's engineering career took his family to Southeast Houston when Von Won was a small child. His household had strong Christian foundations. Von Won recalls attending church multiple nights a week, and even singing in the choir as an adolescent. At the same time, he excelled in both athletics and academics. "Growing up, I was an athlete. I was a straight-A student, and I was in church Sunday and Wednesday nights," he says to summarize his childhood. In high school, he excelled in the long jump and earned a track scholarship to Rice University. The summer before leaving for Rice, he began his lifelong interest in hip hop by forming the Playboy Click, a secular

Figure 12. Von Won at his home in Pasadena, Texas. Photo by author.

rap group with several friends, whom he describes as "a bunch of guys that liked to rap, liked girls, and liked the attention of it all" (interview with the author, July 2012). The Playboy Click's sound was inspired by the mainstream trends at the time but was well immersed in the local screw movement. The group generated a buzz in Houston through the nightclub scene, and he even began working with members of the Screwed Up Click.

As a college student athlete, Von Won continued to enjoy the spoils that came with local rap stardom: money, women, and drugs. At the same time, however, he was active in the local Christian hip hop market, though in a behind-the-scenes way. He assisted a number of Christian hip hop artists, notably including Soldiers on a Mission and Tre-9, with their writing and production. This was an attempt to atone for his engagement in practices that would be considered sinful in Christian contexts. "It was my help to the Lord, while I'm out here trippin'," he says. "It's like at least I'm doin' this for you, Lord; I'm helping these guys out." In 2005, Von Won's father died of AIDS. This event sent him, as he says, "down a bad road." He became depressed, and his drug habit escalated. "I was simply running crazy," he told me. His life changed after another traumatic episode in 2005, and the craziness ceased:

Coming back from a concert, I got stopped by the police in Pearland. It was a bad altercation. I got tased four or five times. I almost died. I almost lost my life. Just after that night, I kind of knew it was time for a change. Ya know? I had my daughter. She was two months old at the time. And this all happened in front of her and my wife, man. It was a bad situation. But after that, I decided to go back to church and get focused. (Interview with the author, July 2012)

After that incident, Von Won recommitted himself to his Christian foundation. His music followed suit: he reoriented his rap persona as a Christian-based artist. Since his awakening, he has become one of the most critically and commercially successful artists in Houston's Christian hip hop scene. In addition, he has become lead pastor of Legacy Church in Houston and an active Christian inspirational speaker.

Both Lil Raskull and Von Won have experience in the Houston streets. Lil Raskull was a Northside drug dealer, and Von Won engaged the streets by way of the secular rap scene. Their personal experiences have inspired them to focus their music-based ministerial efforts on the streets and caused them to feel uniquely able to be effective at this work. Each carefully employs aspects of the secular hip hop tradition as a way to appeal to street-based audiences. They are two among a large base of local artists who take this approach.

CHRISTIAN HIP HOP ARTISTS' ENGAGEMENT WITH SECULAR TRADITION

Christian hip hop artists cautiously embrace Houston's secular hip hop tradition. According to Sketch the Journalist, "they are not ashamed to admit that they grew up listening to DJ Screw, and they still admire and have respect for those guys that laid the groundwork" (interview with the author, 2012). While seldom mentioning syrup, Christian artists often make reference to slabs to bring geographical specificity and cultural pertinence to a song; for example, 007 raps "Jesus Christ necessary like 4's on 'Lacs" on "Someday" from *Audio Future*. Corey Paul's "Don't Give Up" contains the following reference to slab:

A lot of my partnas never make it out of South Park
Galleria tag popping got 'em feeling far
The game raw ironically that's why they cook
riding round in the slab on the dash Good book

Here, Corey Paul refers to slab in conjunction with South Park to make his song acutely relatable to his target audience: people from South Park and other Houston area 'hoods. This audience—the same one courted by secular artists—seeks music with hyperlocal sensibilities. They value songs that address the fine particularities of their social life. References to slab, while seemingly slight, bring Christian songs from a generic space to the specific place, which allows them to have greater resonance among local 'hood- and street-based audiences.

Local Christian rappers commonly collaborate with their secular counterparts, in part because they create songs and stories in a genre that stands in opposition to much of the hardcore thematic content of secular rap. They seek to be germane in the local hip hop culture, and these collaborations with secular artists help bridge that divide. "We feel that it's a way to represent our faith to people that are outside of it," says Sketch. "Even if they don't come to Christ, we are light in the darkness, and we want to be involved in the secular community" (interview with the author, 2012). Lil Raskull, with regard to his collaborations with secular artists, explained, "I have no problem at all. My only qualification is that if you believe Jesus is Lord, then we can jam together" (interview with the author, 2012). Raskull's willingness to work with secular artists is related to his personal history and ideology. He identifies with secular artists and their audiences because of shared experiences. "I came from them guys. I am one of them, just redeemed," he notes. Informed by his personal experiences, he conveys a ministerial message of compassion and understanding. He is firmly committed to Christian principles but does not admonish his peers for exhibiting what some would call spiritual corruptness. Raskull believes that a questionable Christian walk does not preclude one from musically sharing the word of God alongside him.

Lil Raskull displays a fervent willingness to work with secular artists; however, his secular interactions, as he notes, do not occur without caveats: "Now, if you and me make a record, of course, there are certain standards. If it's my record, there are certain things you can say, there are certain things you can't say. It ain't so much as me stifling your creativity or freedom: it's just me knowing my audience and you don't" (interview with the author, July 2012).

Raskull has been open to secular collaborations as long as the resulting music does not compromise his Christian message. In such collaborations, street-based content—explicit language and references to drugs, sex, and violence—is scarce. This is because Lil Raskull "knows his audience," which means two things: first, he does not want to reinforce destructive behavior among his secular audience; second, he wants to present content that his saved and churchgoing core audience would not deem inappropriate.

Raskull's *Good News, Bad Boyz* (2000), a collaboration with local rapper Nuwine, features guest appearances by secular artists Big Hawk, T2, Slaughter, and Papa Ru. Swishahouse emcee Paul Wall appears on "All My Connections," one of the album's more compelling cuts. Nuwine opens the song by detailing his ministerial activity in the streets:

> When I go into them prisons
> And I'm doin' them shows.
> They say, "Nuwine, you sho'll is throwed"

In the verse above, Nuwine says that he ministers to others while wearing a platinum mouth grill. In his next verse, he describes how he "rides on 22, slamming them do's"—a reference to the 22-inch car rims popular on the streets in the early 2000s. He seeks to show that being saved does not prohibit him from engaging in the cultural aspects of the street. Even as a Christian, he can enjoy the clothing, cars, and language of the street while rejecting its destructive elements—drugs, violence, and incarceration. Ultimately, he wants street listeners to understand that, even though he is saved, he is still "one of the homies." Pursuing a Christian walk does not require an outright rejection of local cultural identity.

Similar to Nuwine, Paul Wall exhibits both a street and Christian identity in his verse:

> What it do, It's Paul Wall-ter
> I reinstated my church status
> Now, I'm back speaking out from the altar
> A minister with some street credentials

Here, Paul Wall illuminates the importance of Christian faith in his life. Paul Wall calls himself "a minister with some street credentials," which suggests that he can be one of the chief ambassadors of Houston street practices without compromising his Christian faith. He later attributes much of his career success to his faith when he rhymes, "gave my life to the Lord and watched my career skyrocket." He closes his verse by noting that he rides "in an Impala with a cross around his collar" and "I'm a baller, but I'm still payin' my tithes." The riches that appear to come from his lyrical engagement with the streets are, in his reality, products of his continued bond with God.

Slim Thug, Paul Wall's fellow Swishahouse crew member, appears on "Trouble Don't Last" (2000) with Nuwine and Raskull. On this track, each emcee presents particular challenges that have impacted his life. Nuwine raps about struggling to maintain adherence to Christian principles in the midst of personal strife. His spiritual anxiety causes him to contemplate violent retribution against transgressors, whom he calls haters: "Pump my pistol at a hater, pull the trigger and blast," he raps. Though not explicitly stated, his spiritual anguish appears to stem from a lack of acceptance by his church community, people he calls hypocrites. As demonstrated in his lyrics, the church's lack of compassion for him reflects apathy toward those who come from the street. Ultimately, he chooses to take the Christian route that the church does not, as he realizes that under God's grace, "trouble don't last always." Lil Raskull echoes this theme, too, as in his verse noting everyday trials, such as harassment from bill collectors and others. Such troubles build his spiritual character, proclaiming "trouble for me is like the gym: it makes me hit harder." Slim Thug, in his verse, offers his testimony, detailing his former life of poverty, homelessness, and drug dealing:

> From pushing 'caine to robbin', You name it, I done it
> Claiming money over everything, stackin' my hundreds
> Fallin' back on lawyers, bailing in and outta jail
> A lost soul with no morals, headed to hell.

Slim Thug recognizes his spiritual disconnection as the source of the troubles in his life. He calls himself a "lost soul," whose troubled relationship with God sent him "headed to hell." He was able to reverse the course of his life by "accepting his blessings," which came in the form of rapping. Therefore, as with Paul Wall, Slim Thug attributes his personal and professional success to God's intervention.

Von Won is also known for his collaborations with secular artists. In 2011, he released *One City under God* (2011), his fourth solo album as a Christian artist, to much fanfare. The album features several notable, local Christian hip hop artists, including Bizzle, Gifted, and Dre Murray, as well as Soldiers on a Mission, whom he helped get established in the local hip hop recording industry. Popular songs include "Bow Down," where Von Won expresses his ongoing struggle to subdue his pride and remain focused on praising God, as instructed by his Christian principles. On "Make a Change," he pleads with God to help bring Houston out of the plague of violence and drug abuse.

The signature song of *One City under God* is the title track, a Christian-based city anthem that features mainstream Houston artists Lil O, Lil Keke, Kiotti, and former Christian artist Nuwine. Von Won's verse outlines the spiritual and material riches that come with faith in Christ. He boasts of "giving thanks to the King of All Kings, canary yellow diamonds shining the same color as Yao Ming." He notes having "that Olsteen hope bruh" and suggests that he's "on his way to making history." Secular artists take a different approach on the song. Lil O and Lil Keke of the Screwed Up Click offer testimonies detailing their personal struggles and credit God with helping them overcome. Lil O relates a particular a point in his life when he considered suicide but was saved though faith. Lil Keke mentions that many tests in life had broken his morale, but ultimately notes, "I thank God 'cause he changed my spirit." Nuwine and Kiotti take similar approaches.

Von Won explains that the song "One City under God" was a ministerial move, with the goal of unifying the city under the love of God:

> I always wanted to be this big-time star that travels all around the world, but God really spoke to me and said, "I want you to just focus on Houston"—you know, the 5.9 million people right here in this area. With the One City Under God movement, I want people to really be aware, to take the time to reach out. Not just to people you see in the church, but to everybody, because God created us equal. That's why I reached out to guys like Lil Keke, Kiotti, Nuwine, Lil O, and I said, "Let's come together; let's make some music." (Quoted in Sketch the Journalist 2011)

With *One City under God*, Von Won partnered with secular artists, hoping that the collaboration would inspire unity between Houston's sacred and secular worlds. He felt the city was divided. In his view, churchgoers often isolated themselves from the street and hip hop communities. Hip hoppers and street occupants, in turn, felt judged by churchgoers and naturally distanced themselves from the church. His work with Lil Keke, Lil O, Kiotti, and Nuwine symbolizes the cultural diversity of the church body. The idea of "one city under God" reflects Von Won's hope for a God-fueled synergy between Houston's sacred and secular communities.

Von Won continued this theme on his follow-up album, *Shock Therapy* (2012). This project, which included a book and biographical DVD, offered an open look into Von Won's journey as a man and a Christian. The title is a direct reference to the encounter with the police that changed his life.

Von Won's secular music past is an undeniable aspect of his personal and musical identity. He engages with this history on the track "Elbow Room," which features his former secular group, the Playboy Click. This song stands out from the rest of the album because the Christian content is not overtly expressed. Playboy Click rapper Reese Jones makes the only reference to Christian identity by metaphorically rapping about sipping Jesus's blood by using syrup-related language ("Jesus blood I po' it up / Sip a deuce, fo' it up"). Additionally, Playboy Click rappers refrain from using explicit language and content out of respect for Von Won and his Christian mission, even saying "We gon' try to keep it clean Von." Otherwise, the lyrics follow traditional Houston hip hop themes.

Von Won's performance makes the song particularly interesting. Even though it is his album, his participation on the track is limited to the hook and short, introductory bars before each verse, and they are rooted in Houston hip hop tradition. The hook has elements of a chant, which was the core formula on screw-era choruses. His introductory bars are delivered in a similar manner, and two of them reference Houston hip hop classics. In short, Von Won offers an accurate performance of the Houston hip hop aesthetic. While sparse and rooted in secularity, his performance contributes to his ministerial message. From a testimony standpoint, his acumen in Houston-tinged performance increases the authenticity of his secular history, making his testimony that much more impactful. The stronger message, however, is symbolic: by limiting his participation to these small references to Houston hip hop history, he demonstrates how it is possible to interact with the secular world while retaining Christian sensibilities.

THE COMPLICATION OF CHRISTIAN ENTERTAINMENT

Houston-based Christian artists engage with street culture and local hip hop tradition in their music as a tool of ministry; however, their use of secular content is limited by the music's function as entertainment for churchgoing believers. Lil Raskull speaks to this situation: "We see stuff out here, especially as Black men. We see stuff man, you know. I'm the type of guy to talk about it, but I know that the church don't want to hear it. As long as we're singin' the hymn, we're good. But they don't want to take the blinders off sometimes. So, since I'm trying to keep an audience, I have to be sensitive to that" (interview with the author, July 2012).

Lil Raskull feels that Houston's religious community has, by and large, sought to isolate itself from what it considers the destructive realities of the street and is highly critical of local hip hop subject matter. While the streets are the target of his evangelical mission, the church is his primary consumer base. The church community purchases his records and offers him paid performance opportunities. Therefore, churchgoers' opinion matters, and local Christian rappers must appease them to have success within the scene. As Lil Raskull and others note, this consideration can somewhat limit the reach of their ministerial activity.

The local church community, especially its more conservative segments, remains highly suspicious of Christian rappers' motives. In particular, screw, in name and sound, has a dubious presence within religious spaces: "That name, alone, concerns Christian pastors. They're like 'I'm not letting you play that Screw song in here!' This is especially true when you play it, and it has that slowed-down vocals, and it almost sounds demonic" (Sketch the Journalist, interview with the author, July 2012).

Considering the skepticism of church leaders as well as their desire to persuade audiences, Christian rappers take strategic measures to ensure that their musical messages are clearly communicated. I witnessed this firsthand during Corey Paul's performance at Restoring Hope Church in Webster, Texas, a suburb of Houston, on the evening of June 7, 2012. He performed as part of the church's Focus on the Family concert with fellow Christian rappers Governor and S.O.M., as well as gospel artists Soulfruit and Yunek. Focus on the Family, a youth-oriented concert, drew out many preteens and teens, as well as some of their parents. Corey Paul did something that I had never before seen in a hip hop show: he performed third in the lineup and previewed each song of the set by offering a plainly stated declaration of the song's themes and subject matter. He made sure to communicate the intended meaning of the song before the beat dropped. I later asked him about this practice, and he said, "A lot of my songs have deeper meanings than what you [the listener] may catch. Because the audio may not be crystal clear, you miss certain things; you may lose yourself a lil bit. I like to give the heart of the song before I give you the song, so as I'm doing the song, you'll catch on to it" (interview with the author, July 2012).

Corey Paul offers such introductions to his songs to ensure his meanings are well communicated in spite of sometimes poor church sound systems, which can compromise the clarity of his music. He wants his message to be received in an unambiguous or complicated manner. Sketch the Journalist told me that these practices are common within the Christian hip hop community: "A lot of rappers will perform a cappella or make that a part of their show because a lot of kids come along with their parents, and they want them to clearly hear what they're saying. So parents can know that they are good and safe and have a spiritual message that they can agree with" (interview with the author, 2012).

Despite their attempts to communicate their spiritual motives, Christian rappers continue to have complicated relationships with local churches. Many churches are hesitant to allow the performance of Christian rap in their spaces. When Christian rap is brought into the church, it is typically relegated to youth-related events, and poor sound engineering and wary church leadership compromise these performances. Nevertheless, Christian rappers are compelled to continue to court the attention of church bodies because they contribute a large portion of their consumer base.

HIP HOP MISSIONARIES: CREATING SACRED SPACE IN THE STREETS

Many local Christian rappers are involved in traditional ministries that involve physical interaction with both Christian and non-Christian communities. Andre "007" Barnes founded "Taking Back the Streets," a ministry through which he organizes faith-centered charity events and performances around Houston. Corey Paul and his Frontline Movement bring Christian hip hop into prisons and group homes. Von Won is lead pastor at Legacy Church in Houston. Hip hop music is part of the communicative foundation of each ministry, as it continues to be an effective way to connect to targeted congregations.

In a similar vein is local artist Tre-9, who has collaborated with secular artists such as Bun B of UGK and S.U.C. members Big Hawk and Lil Keke. Tre-9, however, has gone a step further by creating multiple spaces that offer discursive and physical alternatives to the streets. He considers himself a hip hop missionary: "I don't just sit in a church pew on Sunday," he says. "I actually use the influence of hip hop to do strategic and effective ministry, missions, evangelism, discipleship wherever it's needed" (interview with the author, 2012). Over the course of his career, he has been involved in the creation of several physical and virtual institutions, including Much Luvv Records, DaSouth.com, and Hip Hop Hope Missions, all of which further his missionary goals.

Tre-9, born Bobby Herring, was raised in a two-parent household in a predominantly Hispanic area in the Northside. Though as a White youth he was a minority in his neighborhood, he built social capital through his skills on the basketball court. In fifth grade, he became enamored with hip hop after visiting nearby Moody Park, where he witnessed an impromptu performance by local break dancers and emcees. He eventually moved from consumer to practitioner and began writing his own raps based on the popular trends at the time. "I was rapping about sex, drugs, violence, 'I'll shoot you,'" he conveyed to me. "I was regurgitating everything I heard, which is what most people do today anyway" (interview with the author, July 2012).

Tre-9 did not grow up in a Christian household. His mother visited church from time to time, but his father never attended at all. At age 18, Tre-9 did not have much of a relationship with God. His radical change after high school is due to a gig running sound for churches: "While I was there setting up sound for the church, I would listen to the pastor speak. And I would begin to ask questions. Before you knew it, I kind of fell in love with the word of God, and from that point on, I never looked back" (interview with the author, July 2012).

This major change in Tre-9's life prompted a radical reorientation of his lyrical content. He went from glorifying the streets to critiquing them. This was not the result of some spiritual directive, however: it was based on his desire for his music to be a better reflection of who he was as a person. "I was learning new things," he says. "I was growing, and I found new things to rap about." He hesitated to embrace Christian rap at first, preferring to make what he calls "positive" rap. But he would soon come to embrace his growing Christian foundations:

> You know, I don't remember having a moment where I was like, "I gotta be real now"—because I was a baby Christian. I remember saying to myself, "I'm gonna be positive," because Christian rap was corny, but when you take on a new life, it'd be like if I moved to a foreign country and I adapted their customs and I learned their ways: I'm gonna be rapping about that lifestyle. Ya know? Not America's this, or America's that. If I'm living in Africa, I'm gonna be rapping about my surroundings in Africa because that'll relate to the people. So when I became a Christian and I began to grow and study, learn the word, and learn what God expected, that's what came out of me. I knew it was a contradiction to write about what I was before. And what I was learning in the Bible was that you don't promote evil: you don't let evil come out your mouth. So I had to make a change, but at the same time, the change was a reflection of my new life. (Interview with the author, July 2012)

Inspired by his new Christian walk, Tre-9's lyricism became grounded in biblical teachings. He was a full-fledged Christian rapper. His earliest works grapple with the unfortunate outcomes of street life and offer support for those who desire to distance themselves from it. This marked the beginning of his life as a hip hop missionary. Inspired by his Christian life, he began using the medium of rap music to uplift others.

Although Tre-9 embraced his Christian rapper identity in 1995, the Houston hip hop scene had no infrastructure for Christian rap at that time. Most importantly, no record labels would provide him with the creative and financial support necessary to spread his message. Embracing Houston hip hop culture's independent spirit, he decided to start his own label to release his music, establishing Much Luvv Records in 1998. Until its dissolution in 2012, Much Luvv Records released more than seventeen Christian hip hop albums and was a vital sacred space for artists who sought to distance themselves from the trappings of secular hip hop. Record labels have long been understood as media for subcultural activity. Stax Records, for example, was an important vehicle of Black power ideology and action in the 1960s and 1970s, and the same can be said of indie labels such as Dischord and SST for punks in the 1980s. On a smaller and more directed scale, Much Luvv

Figure 13. Tre-9 in front of DaSouth.com trailer. Photo by author.

has been a vital cog in Houston's hip hop evangelical movement. Aside from Tre-9, Von Won, 007, and Gifted the Flamethrowa are among the notable Christian artists who released albums through the label. Much Luvv also released *Testimony to My Redemption* (2009), former Geto Boy Bushwick Bill's foray into Christian rap. Much Luvv Records provided space for the production and dissemination of their particular version of Christian ideology through rap.

Since closing Much Luvv, Tre-9 has focused on hip hop missionary work. He mentors youth and young adults who seek to move away from destructive lifestyles and toward a Christ-centered worldview. White rapper Pyrexx is a shining example of his missionary work. Known for his spitfire delivery of lyrics detailing street life, Pyrexx began his career as a member of Trae tha Truth's Assholes By Nature (ABN) crew in the 2000s. Pyrexx was in the middle of a ten-year prison term when he met Tre-9, who was engaged in prison ministry. Pyrexx was impressed by Tre-9's Christian rap, and the two began corresponding about his spiritual turmoil, which was rooted in his mother's then-recent death. Pyrexx resumed his secular rap career upon his release from prison in 2011, but Tre-9 continued to urge him to change his life. After triumphantly appearing on Trae tha Truth's popular single "Strapped Up," Pyrexx took a downward turn, as his relationship with ABN dissolved and he ended up back in prison.

Pyrexx was paroled in early 2011 and, after continued mentoring from Tre-9, he fully committed himself to Christ. He now travels around the Houston area, sharing his testimony to young children and adults with the hope that he can steer them away from the mistakes that he made. In 2013, he made his Christian hip hop debut as a guest on Tre-9's "Show Me Your Way," which creatively portrays their relationship. Pyrexx has since become a full-fledged Christian rapper, whose debut album, *Born Again Disciple*, was released on Houston-based Rapture Records in 2015.

Tre-9's discipleship work with Pyrexx is done on a larger scale through his Hip Hop Hope Mission, which he founded with the purpose of using "hip hop culture to build the Body of Christ." Hip Hop Hope began in Fifth Ward, but has branched out to other locations within the city. One such area is Brookshire, a suburb ten miles west of downtown Houston. According to Tre-9, Brookshire youth were facing a multitude of social issues, and this inspired his intervention: "They had two suicides and twenty drug overdoses amongst their high school students within a span of sixty days. So they asked if we'd come help, Hip Hop Hope. And so as a missionary, I go in, look at the demographic, look at the problems, ya know, look at the culture and environment, look at the church, see what they're doin', and then develop a strategic plan in order to reach those people and point those kids in the right direction" (interview with the author, July 2012).

Tre-9's plan was to use hip hop culture as a medium through which to restore hope in the kids. Every Thursday night is Hip Hop Hope Thursday, an event that features live Christian hip hop performances, games, evangelizing, and general fellowship among participants. It is supported by in-school activities and a mentorship program. Tre-9 has taken Hip Hop Hope outside of Texas as well, spending extended time in Chicago and São Paolo, Brazil.

Houston street culture impacts the music-making practices of local Christian hip hop artists. Rather than a catalyst for creativity, however, the streets are targets of ministry. Accordingly, these artists view Houston hip hop heritage as a resource that can help their ministerial efforts in the streets. Artists like 007, Corey Paul, and Von Won use local hip hop identity as an evangelical bridge that allows their messages to penetrate the relatively impervious boundaries of the street. Christian hip hop artists collaborate with popular local secular artists to achieve the same effect. Ultimately, the work of these Houston-based Christian rappers illustrates the power and pervasiveness of Houston's hip hop tradition.

CONCLUSION

Heritage is not a static state. It does not simply appear out of nowhere and attach itself to cultural practices. Heritage is a process that is actively produced and reproduced through social interaction. Over the course of this book, we have discussed how Houston hip hop heritage is reciprocally connected to African American Houstonians' embodiment of space and place. The screw music, slabs, and lean all emerged out of the street and became synthesized into a heritage through local artists' desire to rep their 'hoods both locally and on a national level. In turn, this heritage impacts local music-making practices. For some, Houston hip hop heritage gives their music direction and meaning. Their musical mission is to rep their 'hood by staying true to the heritage. Others have a more complicated view. They see value in the heritage, but it can be difficult to stay true to the city while staying true to yourself. Over the course of several chapters, we have explored a musical community's hyperlocally cultivated soundscape, lyrical themes, and subcultural forms from the perspective of those members of the scene; that is, to make musical sense of what the practitioners define as their music and their heritage beyond the assumptions attached to the culture by the most obvious, crossover artists and the misappropriation of the subculture by mainstream consumers.

Local hip hop heritage is a source of empowerment. Whereas oil, cowboys, and the space program are markers of locality within mainstream Houston, "screw" reflects working-class Black Houston's sense of place. The "City of

Syrup" and "Screwston" monikers reflect the function of screw as the Black working class's intracommunity-defined conception of the city. Furthermore, screw has offered Houston artists and audiences their own unique identity within a national hip hop landscape rooted in local and regional expressions. There has been a resolute and intergenerational embrace of screw revealing that its meaning goes beyond recreation; it is a form of intangible cultural heritage. Within Houston, hip hop is art, tradition, and lived experience for a community of people consciously seeking self-sufficiency and self-definition.

This project was very personal in nature. As I explained in the introduction to this book, I was born and raised in Houston, in the very same Black neighborhoods that many of my hip hop friends emerged from. Like them, I played at MacGregor Park as a child. Timmy Chan's and Navy Seafood were regular Friday night cuisines for my family. Magic 102.1, 97.9 the Box, and 90.9 KTSU provided the soundtrack in my household. My Black Houston roots are very deep. My dad was raised on the Southside and my mother on the North. I had the best of both worlds in some sense. With every interview that I conducted came a sense of shared experience and sometimes shared struggle.

But I moved away from Houston when I was eighteen years old. I spent four years in Austin, Texas, working on a bachelor's degree at the University of Texas. Then I moved to Bloomington, Indiana, for many years in pursuit of my masters and eventually my doctorate degrees. This distance created a void in me. I missed home. Not just my family and friends, the Black folk culture of the area. Houston hip hop, being so grounded in hyperlocal references, helped fill that void. It was a way for me to feel Houston, feel the Southside, and feel Hiram Clarke even in my state of dislocation.

While in the field, I negotiated a hybrid identity: part local boy and part researcher. Some of the time I felt like a cultural insider writing about his community. At other times, I was very self-aware of my outsider-ness. I had not lived in the city for over a decade and, as a result, my sense of home was a bit more complex. Further, I was also a researcher whose goal was to collect data for a project that would fulfill degree requirements for a university one thousand miles away. I felt like I was taking from the community or exploiting it in some way.

Like the hip hop artists I worked with, I was also driven by the impulse to rep' my 'hood in my own way. I immediately saw potential in slab culture.

I did not enter the field intending to devote significant time to studying the culture. But as time went on, I found myself giving more and more attention to slab. In late March 2012, I was invited to moderate a panel on slab at the Awwready: Houston Hip Hop Conference at the University of Houston. University archivist Julie Grob, who was actively building a local hip hop collection at the university's archive, organized the event. Moderating this panel inspired me to dig deeper into the culture. OG Scott and the Bloc Boyz Click were immensely helpful in this regard. They schooled me to the ins and outs of the culture and kept me informed about slab-related events. These experiences helped me recognize slab as a truly complex and captivating art form that was worthy of public exploration and celebration.

A parade made the most sense. Processional was already a core part of slab practice, and I figured that it would easily translate into something more elaborate. Since I grew up in a predominantly Black neighborhood in the city, I also knew that parades had an important place in local Black culture. The two Martin Luther King Jr. Day parades and the Texas Southern University Homecoming parade have long been sources of great joy and cultural pride within the community. Therefore I figured that a parade of slabs would be culturally resonant.

The slab parade was political in nature. Houston has long touted itself as one of America's most diverse cities. This is true in many ways. The city's non-White population is both robust and varied. I was proud to have been able to attend school with Asian Americans, African Immigrants, Jewish folks, Mexican Americans, and White Americans along with my fellow African Americans. The story was quite different outside of school grounds, however. Houston, like other cities, is structured by severe residential segregation. An analysis from *FiveThirtyEight* found Houston to be one of the United States' most segregated cities (Silver 2015). While racism amongst the city's inhabitants is certainly a factor, segregation in the city is not solely de facto in nature. In 2017, the United States Department of Housing and Urban Development found that the City of Houston was in violation of Title VI of the Civil Rights Act due to housing practices that purposely facilitate racial segregation (Elliott 2017). *FiveThirtyEight* and HUD only confirmed what non-White Houstonians had long felt: that Houston has a segregation problem.

Racial segregation has a large effect on African American life in Houston. Black Houstonians continue to be among the most segregated communities in Houston. A 2016 Kinder Institute study titled "The Shifting City: Houston's History of Unequal Racial Change" notes that the influx of non-White Hispanics has radically reoriented demographics in the city. These trends have more than quadrupled the number of neighborhoods that are racially diverse, where no single group is in the majority. However, these areas are largely in the suburbs. The inner city, where African Americans generally live, remains mostly unchanged. Neighborhoods that were segregated thirty years ago continue to be so today. This racial segregation has major implications on the high levels of poverty, unemployment, and disenfranchisement among local Blacks. Racial segregation also has a major impact on Houston's cultural sector. Houston's African American culture is robust and multifaceted. The art forms, practices, and institutions remain isolated, however, crushed by the weight of cultural hegemony. I witnessed this firsthand as my father navigated the racial dynamics of the local theater and musical arts scenes.

Local hip hop culture has made a major impact around the nation and around the world. Yet it has not received its proper respect within the city.

A form of heritage must be safeguarded or protected from threats to its vitality. Common threats include migration, policy, economics, or simply the passage of time. Slab needed safeguarding from the racist perceptions about its primary Black male participant base. Many Houstonians saw slab as a mark of gangsterism, a rolling reflection of inner-city materialism and violence. Folklorist Michelle Stefano writes that safeguarding heritage includes the "necessity to disrupt and, thereby, change the status quo, no matter how small the intervention" (2022, 4). In my mind, the slab parade could be an unapologetic celebration of African American and hip hop culture in Houston. It would, at least for a moment, bring the margins to the mainstream. These young working-class Black men and women would, at least for a moment, be recognized for their creativity instead of stereotyped by their supposed criminalization. Houston hip hop would be finally recognized as the complex, imaginative, and influential culture it is within its city of origin.

Stefano further notes that safeguarding cultural heritage is not a solo endeavor and can only be done "through truly collaborative and equitable efforts" (2022, 4). A cross-cultural coalition of culture workers, social institutions, artists, and slab riders collaborated to organize the parade. I first brought the idea of the parade to OG Scott. While I thought it was a good idea, I wanted to make sure that members of the slab and hip hop community were in support of it. I wanted the ideas, desires, and concerns of the community to be centered throughout this entire process. OG Scott had been a figure in both scenes for many years and had his finger on the pulse of the community. Plus, he and the Bloc Boyz Click were my primary connection to the slab community, and I felt that they would be able to gauge the slab community's interest in such an event. OG Scott responded enthusiastically to the idea and committed to getting the community involved. I took the idea to Pat Jasper, director of Folk and Traditional Arts at the Houston Arts Alliance (HAA) and John Guess, then director and CEO of the Houston Museum of African American Culture (HMAAC). At the time, I had been working at a co-fellowship between these two organizations, where I documented traditional artists within Houston's African Diasporic community. Both institutions quickly got on board. This was a risky move for both organizations, considering the cultural conservatism of mainstream Houston. But they embraced the vision and provided invaluable institutional infrastructure. Navigating Houston's political and cultural environmental would have been impossible without their involvement.

With the HMAAC and HAA as well as City Council District D providing funding resources and an institutional base, slab community insiders like the Bloc Boyz Click, rapper Paul Wall, customizer B.G., slab rider Fourth Ward Fish, and documentarian Meyagi worked tirelessly to cultivate slab community support and participation. They used their personal relationships to help plan the event, market it within the community, and register participants. This allowed the community to retain ownership and control while, at the same time, accessing the resources and infrastructure of these civic institutions.

The Houston Slab Parade & Family Festival took place on October 20, 2013, in MacGregor Park. The parade portion began at King's Flea Market, which had recently ceased operations. With kid cyclists from Workshop Houston, a local nonprofit, leading the way, fifty cars paraded from King's to MacGregor Park. A single line of cars drove into the park at a sluggish pace, aided only by the mishmash of hip hop sounds coming from their powerful stereo systems. The cars situated themselves in an orderly, color-coded fashion in a reserved section in the park's northwest corner. There were sections for red cars, blue cars, green cars, teal cars, and gold cars, and a separate section for cars of other assorted colors. A mini-festival followed the parade. Local icon MC Wickett Crickett, who died in 2015, hosted the event. Hip hop artists such as E.S.G., K-Rino, and Yungstar performed. Dance teams and poets also

Figure 14. E.S.G. and son performing at the Houston Slab Parade & Family Festival. Photo by author.

performed while local street arts created live works. Area vendors promoted and sold their products and services.

As I have written before, slab is a street-based practice and its relevance within local hip hop culture has been largely cultivated by street-based artists. However, other hip hop communities were very present at the event. Underground artist Bishop Black and Christian hip hop writer Sketch the Journalist were among the spectators that day.

Since the parade, slab has taken on a larger space in Houston's cultural landscape. In 2015, slab rider P Izm, rapper Bun B of UGK, and I represented slab and hip hop culture on an episode of *Booze Traveler*, a Travel Channel television show that explored alcoholic beverage practices and cultural traditions in various United States cities. The episode positioned slab and screw as central traditions within Houston's cultural landscape. Moving between a drive-thru margarita shop and popular 8th Wonder Brewery, P Izm drove host Jack Maxwell and me in his white slab as we discussed the ins and outs of the tradition. In addition, popular television show *Anthony Bourdain: Parts Unknown* featured slabs in a Houston-based episode in 2016.

In 2015, then–Houston Mayor Anise Parker rode in a slab during the 2015 Art Car Parade. Founded in 1988, the Houston Art Car Parade is an annual

Figure 15. Slabs at the Houston Slab Parade & Family Festival. Photo by author.

event that celebrates various types of vehicle art. Reflecting the cultural isolation of slab and working-class African American life in Houston, the Art
Car Parade had never featured slabs in its twenty-seven-year history even
though slabs are, by definition, art cars. Slabs' inclusion in the parade, along
with the mayor riding in one, reflects its movement from the margins to the
mainstream. Black working-class cultural expression is now being integrated
into Houston's cultural fabric.

In the near-decade since I conducted the bulk of my fieldwork, Houston's
hip hop scene has continued to be locally vibrant. Musically, younger artists
like OMB Bloodbath, Don Tolliver, and Sauce Walka continue to build upon
the foundations set by scene elders. On a cultural level, Houston hip hop
artists have more of a presence in mainstream Houston. Bun B has acquired
an incredible level of crossover appeal to the point that some call him the
"Unofficial Mayor of Houston." Trae tha Truth has received much praise for
his Relief Gang organization, which saved many lives during Hurricane Harvey in 2017. The scene is also having a renewed national impact. South Park
native Megan Thee Stallion is one of the most popular rappers in the world.
She is dominating pop culture with her sharp flow and lyrics that center Black
womanhood and sexual agency. Southwest Houston's Travis Scott has built
a cult following with his lo-fi sounds, trippy lyrics, and collaborations with

Figure 16. Langston Collin Wilkins and TV Johnny at the Houston Slab Parade & Family Festival. Photo by author.

Drake, Kanye West, and others. Former athlete Tobe Nwigwe has galvanized audiences by making some of the most accessible abstract rap of our time. Despite reaching incredible commercial and cultural heights, these artists continued to remain grounded in Houston's hip hop heritage.

Segregation, poverty, unemployment, and crime create an oppressive storm that has victimized Black working-class Houston. This is a crushing oppression that seeks to marginalize, isolate, and terminate. But the community is resilient. Lacking resources, they turn to the 'hood as a source of empowerment. There are no prerequisites to owning the 'hood. Your apartment building, street, or even the city itself becomes your birthright. You protect it and you champion it. It is a way for these individuals, living in a constant state of precariousness and isolation, to feel less alone in the world. Local hip hop culture synthesizes, articulates, reinforces, and celebrates the meanings generated from the bond between people and place. Black Houstonians turned Houston into *Screwston*, crystallizing a cultural heritage that will continue to protect, affirm, and inspire locals for years to come.

NOTES

CHAPTER 1. IF YOU GO DOWN TO HOUSTON

Epigraph 1: Bonner, Weldon "Jukeboy." 1968. "Stay Off Lyons Avenue." *I'm Going Back to the Country Where They Don't Burn the Buildings Down*. Arhoolie Records.

Epigraph 2: Guerilla Maab. 1999. "Fondren and Main." *Rise*. Resurrection Music Group.

1. Screwed Up Records & Tapes was located at 7717 Cullen Blvd. in South Park before moving to Hiram Clarke in 2012.

CHAPTER 3. STILL TIPPIN'

1. Hinojosa, Jorge, dir. 2012. *Iceburg Slim: Portrait of a Pimp*. Documentary. Final Level Entertainment/United Talent Agency.

CHAPTER 4. GOTTA COME DOWN, GOTTA REP THE HOOD

Epigraph: Block Boyz Click. 2013. "Purple Swag (S.U.C. Houston Edition)." Single. Cloverland Records.

1. A "roll call" is a verbal art practice in which an individual offers a colorful salutation toward people and places that are of importance to them.

2. 9 Months Later, Still a G at 23, Wreckshop, Freestyle Kingz, June 27, Southside Still Holdin', and 3 n the Mornin' are popular DJ Screw mixtapes.

3. Fat Pat, Big Moe, Big Hawk (Dub-K), Big Steve, and DJ Screw are deceased members of the Screwed Up Click. Fat Pat, Big Hawk, and DJ Screw were members of the Dead End Alliance (D.E.A.), a subgroup of the S.U.C.

4. Barre was a popular brand of codeine cough syrup in Houston. "Barre" is now a reference to generic syrup.

5. "Four" means four ounces of cough syrup.

CHAPTER 5. TURNIN' HEADZ

1. Aesop Rock is a New York–based emcee, known for his cryptic lyrics and unorthodox vocal style.

2. Boom-bap is a hip hop production style that emerged in New York in the early 1990s. It is characterized by prominent bass-drum sounds and samples from funk, jazz, and soul sources. It is lyrically diverse, but commonly rooted in East Coast street life.

3. Horrorcore is a style of hip hop characterized by the use of horror movie themes in lyrics.

4. Wu-Tang Clan is a popular New York–based hip hop group that emerged in the early 1990s.

5. D-Risha. 2012. "Save the Day." *Big Trouble in Houston, Texas*. Self-released.

CHAPTER 6. ONE CITY UNDER GOD

1. *Word*, as used by Barnes, refers to the Word of God, understood to be Christian principles based on the Holy Bible.

References

Agee-Aldridge, Jenny. 2014. "Houston's 5th Ward Redevelopment Continues with Plans for Single-Family Homes." *Houston Business Journal*, February 27, 2014. https://www.bizjournals.com/houston/morning_call/2014/02/houstons-fifth-ward-redevelopment-efforts-continue.html.

Agnew, John. 2011. "Space and Place." In *The Handbook of Geographical Knowledge*, edited by John Agnew and David N. Livingstone, 316–30. Thousand Oaks, Calif.: Sage Publications.

Anderson, Elijah. 1999. *Code of the Street: Decency, Violence, and the Moral Life of the Inner City*. New York: Norton.

Baker-Fletcher, Garth Kasimu. 2003. "African American Christian Rap: Facing 'Truth' and Resisting It." In *Noise and Spirit: The Religious Sensibilities of Rap Music*, edited by Anthony B. Pinn, 29–48. New York: NYU Press.

Barnes, Sandra L. 2008. "Religion and Rap Music: An Analysis of Black Church Usage." *Review of Religious Research* 49 (2): 319–38.

Beeth, Howard, and Cary D. Wintz. 1992. *Black Dixie: Afro-Texan History and Culture in Houston*. College Station: Texas A&M Press.

Bennett, Andy. 2015. "Popular Music and the 'Problem' of Heritage." In *Sites of Popular Music Heritage: Memories, Histories, Place*, edited by Sara Cohen, Robert Knifton, Marion Leonard, and Les Roberts. New York: Routledge.

Bohlman, Philip V. 1988. *The Study of Folk Music in the Modern World*. Bloomington: Indiana University Press.

Boney, Jefferey L. 2013. "Black Business Is Black History! The *Houston Forward Times* Highlights Three History-Making Houston Businesses." *Houston Forward Times*, February 20, 2013. http://forwardtimesonline.com/index.php?option=com_content&view=article&id=1641.

Boyd, Todd. 2007. *The Notorious Phd's Guide to the Super Fly '70s: A Connoisseur's Journey Through the Fabulous Flix, Hip Sounds, and Cool Vibes That Defined a Decade*. New York: Crown.

Bradley, Regina. 2021. *Chronicling Stankonia: The Rise of the Hip Hop South*. Chapel Hill: University of North Carolina Press.

Bray, Daika. 1999. "DJ Screw." *Murder Dog Magazine*, August 1999. www.murder dog.com/archives/djscrew/djscrew.html. Accessed March 2, 2013.

Brown, Barbara, Douglas D. Perkins, and Graham Brown. 2003. "Place Attachment in a Revitalizing Neighborhood: Individual and Block Levels of Analysis." *Journal of Environmental Psychology* 23 (3): 259–71.

Brown, Ernest D., Jr. 2015. "African American Instrument Construction and Music Making." In *African American Music: An Introduction*, edited by Mellonee V. Burnim and Portia K. Maultsby, 23–33. New York: Routledge.

Bullard, Robert D. 1987. *Invisible Houston: The Black Experience in Boom and Bust*. College Station: Texas A&M Press.

Bullock, Henry J. 1957. *Pathways to the Houston Negro Market*. Ann Arbor: J. W. Edwards.

Chisholm, Diane. 2005. *Queer Constellations: Subcultural Space in the Wake of the City*. Minneapolis: University of Minnesota Press.

City of Houston. 2012. "Race/Ethnicity: City of Houston by Super Neighborhoods." http://www.houstontx.gov/planning/Demographics/docs_pdfs/SN/sn_coh_race _ethn.pdf. Accessed January 17, 2015.

———. 2013a. "Employment Status for the Popular 16 Years and Over: City of Houston by Super Neighborhood." http://www.houstontx.gov/planning/Demographics/ docs_pdfs/SN/Employment%20Status%20by%20SN.pdf. Accessed January 17, 2014.

———. 2013b. "Median Household Income: City of Houston by Super Neighborhoods." http://www.houstontx.gov/planning/Demographics/docs_pdfs/SN/Median _Household_Income_by_SN.pdf. Accessed January 12, 2015.

de-Miguel-Molina, Blanca, and Rafael Boix-Domenech. 2021. "Introduction: Music, from Intangible Cultural Heritage to the Music Industry." In *Music as Intangible Cultural Heritage: Economic, Cultural and Social Identity*, edited by Blanca de-Miguel-Molina, Virginia Santamarina-Campos, Maria de-Miguel-Molina, and Rafael Boix-Domenech, 3–7. Cham, Switzerland: SpringerBriefs in Economics.

Duggins, Kamilah. 2000. "Third Ward Rebound." *Houston Press*, November 16, 2000. http://www.houstonpress.com/2000-11-16/news/third-ward-rebound/.

Eaton, Collin. 2016. "1980s Oil Bust Left a Lasting Mark." *Houston Chronicle*, August 31, 2016. https://www.chron.com/local/history/economy-business/article/ The-1980s-oil-bust-left-lasting-mark-on-Houston-9195222.php.

Elliott, Rebecca. 2017. "HUD: City's Subsidized Housing Procedures Promote Segregation, Violate Civil Rights Act." *Houston Chronicle*, January 13, 2017. https://www .houstonchronicle.com/politics/houston/article/HUD-City-s-subsidized-housing -procedures-promote-10857101.php.

Elwood, William N. 2001. "Sticky Business: Patterns of Procurement and Misuse of Prescription Cough Syrup in Houston." *Journal of Psychoactive Drugs* 33 (3): 121–33.

Emery, Andrew. 2013. "Lil' Wayne's Seizures: Is Cough Syrup the Cause?" *The Guardian*, March 26, 2013. http://www.theguardian.com/theguardian/shortcuts/2013/mar/26/lil-wayne-cough-syrup-seizures. Accessed February 25, 2015.

Farrugia, Rebekah, and Kellie D. Hay. 2017. "Wrecking Rap's Conventions: The Cultural Production of Three Daring Detroit Emcees." *Popular Music* 37 (1): 63–80.

Forman, Murray. 2002. *The 'Hood Comes First: Race, Space, and Place in Rap and Hip-Hop.* Middletown, Conn.: Wesleyan University Press.

Frere-Jones, Sasha. 2005. "A Place in the Sun." *New Yorker*, November 6, 2005. https://www.newyorker.com/magazine/2005/11/14/a-place-in-the-sun.

Gidal, Marc Meistrich. 2014. "Musical Boundary-Work: Ethnomusicology, Symbolic Boundary Studies, and Music in the Afro-Gaucho Religious Community of Southern Brazil." *Ethnomusicology* 58 (1): 83–109.

Gifford, Justin. 2013. *Pimping Fictions: African American Crime Literature and the Untold Story of Black Pulp Publishing.* Philadelphia: Temple University Press.

Gilroy, Paul. 2001. "Driving While Black." In *Car Culture*, edited by Daniel Miller, 81–104. New York: Oxford.

Gonzales, Michael. 2007. "Cashmere Thoughts." In *Beats, Rhymes, and Life: What We Love and Hate about Hip Hop*, edited by Kenji Jasper and Ytasha Womack, 101–25. New York: Random House.

Gordon, Fon L. 2017. "Early Motoring in Florida: Making Car Culture and Race in the New South, 1903–1943." *Florida Historical Quarterly* 95 (4): 517–37.

Hall, Michael. 2001. "The Slow Life and Fast Death of DJ Screw." *Texas Monthly*, April 2001. http://www.texasmonthly.com/story/slow-life-and-fast-death-dj-screw.

Harrison, Anthony Kwame. 2009. *Hip Hop Underground: The Integrity and Ethics of Racial Imagination.* Philadelphia: Temple University Press.

Haymes, Stephen Nathan. 1995. *Race, Culture, and the City: A Pedagogy for Black Urban Struggle.* Albany: State University of New York.

Head, James. 2010. "Bonner, Weldon Philip H. [Juke Boy]." *Handbook of Texas Online.* http://www.tshaonline.org/handbook/online/articles/fboak. Accessed March 25, 2015.

Hidalgo, M. Carmen, and Bernardo Hernandez. 2001. "Place Attachment: Conceptual and Empirical Questions." *Journal of Environmental Psychology* 21 (3): 273–81.

Horwitz, Sari. 2012. "George Zimmerman Charged with Second-degree Murder in Trayvon Martin Shooting." *Washington Post*, April 11, 2012. http://www.washingtonpost.com/politics/george-zimmerman-to-be-charged-in-trayvon-martin-shooting-law-enforcement-official-says/2012/04/11/gIQAHJ50AT_story.html.

Howard, Jay R., and John M. Streck. 1999. *Apostles of Rock: The Splintered World of Contemporary Christian Music.* Lexington: University of Kentucky.

Jeffries, Michael P. 2011. *Thug Life: Race, Gender, and the Meaning of Hip-Hop.* Chicago: University of Chicago Press.

Johnson, John H. 1949. "Why Negroes Buy Cadillacs." *Ebony*, September 1949.

Kinder Institute for Social Research. 2016. "The Shifting City: Houston's History of Unequal Racial Change." June 1, 2016. https://kinder.rice.edu/research/shifting -city-houstons-unequal-history-racial-change.

Kirshenblatt-Gimblett, Barbara. 1995. "Theorizing Heritage." *Ethnomusicology* 39 (3): 367–80.

Kobza, Crystal. 2012. "Man Killed When Gunfire Erupts at Vigil for Shooting Victim." *Abc13.com*, May 4, 2012. http://abc13.com/archive/8647961/.

Latham, Aaron. 1985. "The Return of the Urban Cowboy." *Texas Monthly*, November 1985.

Lefebvre, Henri. 1991. *The Production of Space*. Maiden: Blackwell.

Lynch, Jamie. 2009. "The Long, Hot Grind: How Houston Engineered an Industry of Independence." In *Hip Hop in America: A Regional Guide*, edited by Mickey Hess, 429–66. Santa Barbara: Greenwood Press.

Macdonald, David. 2009. "Carrying Words Like Weapons: Hip-hop and the Poetics of Palestinian Identities in Israel." *Min-Ad: Israeli Studies in Musicology Online* 7 (2): 116–30.

Markman, Rob. 2012. "A$AP Rocky Addresses Kanye West Producer's Criticism." *MTV.com*, May 23. http://www.mtv.com/news/1685714/asap-rocky-mike-dean -criticism/.

Martin, Florian. 2019. "Greenspoint Is Undergoing Major Changes but It's Not Quite Houston's New Hotspot Just Yet." *Houston Public Media*, May 31, 2019. https:// www.houstonpublicmedia.org/articles/news/2019/05/31/335110/greenspoint-is -undergoing-major-changes-but-its-not-quite-houstons-new-hotspot-just-yet/.

Massey, Doreen. 1995. "The Conceptualization of Place." In *A Place in the World*. Milton Keynes: The Open University.

Maultsby, Portia K. 2005. "Africanisms in African American Music." In *Africanisms in American Culture*, edited by Joseph E. Holloway, 326–52. Bloomington: Indiana University.

Meadows-Ingram, Benjamin. 2005. "Sittin' Pretty." *Vibe Magazine*, January 2005.

Merida, Kevin. 1999. "A New Spin on a Golden Oldie." *Washington Post*. January 1, 1999.

Morgan, Marcyliena. 2009. *The Real Hip Hop: Battling for Knowledge, Power, and Respect in the LA Underground*. Durham: Duke University Press.

Morrison, Craig. 2000. "Psychedelic Music in San Francisco: Style, Context, and Evolution." PhD diss., Concordia University. http://spectrum.library.concordia .ca/1163/. Accessed February 25, 2015.

Myers, Margaret, and Sharon G. Dean. 2007. "'Cadillac Flambé': Race and Brand Identity." *Charm* 13: 157–61.

Neff, Ali Colleen. 2011. *Let the World Listen Right: The Mississippi Delta Hip Hop Story*. Jackson: University of Mississippi Press.

Oliver, William. 2006. "The Streets: An Alternative Black Male Socialization Institution." *Journal of Black Studies* 36: 918–37.

Peters, Ronald J., Steven H. Kelder, George S. Yacoubian, LeCresha A. Peters, and Artist Ellis. 2003. "Beliefs and Social Norms about Codeine and Promethazine Hydrochloride Cough Syrup (CPHCS) Onset and Perceived Addiction among Urban Houstonian Adolescents: An Addiction Trend in the City of Lean." *Journal of Drug Education* 33 (4): 415–25.

Petrusich, Amanda. 2014. "Jam Nuthin' but That Screw." *Oxford American*, December 1, 2014. http://www.oxfordamerican.org/magazine/item/509-jam-nothin-but-that -screw. Accessed November 12, 2015.

QDIII, exec. prod. 2007. *Beef IV*. DVD. Image Entertainment.

Quinn, E. 2001. "Pimpin' Ain't Easy: Work, Play, and the Lifestylization of the Black Pimp Figure in Early 1970s Black America." In *Media, Culture and the Modern African American Freedom Struggle*, edited by Brian Ward, 211–32. Gainesville: University of Florida.

———. 2005. *Nuthin' but a "G" Thang: The Culture and Commerce of Gangsta Rap.* New York: Columbia University Press.

Reid, Shaheem. 2008. "Lil Wayne on Syrup: 'Everybody Wants Me to Stop . . . It Ain't That Easy.'" *MTV News*, February 28. http://www.mtv.com/news/1582520/ lil-wayne-on-syrup-everybody-wants-me-to-stop-it-aint-that-easy/.

Reinarman, Craig, and Harry G. Levine. 1997. *Crack in America: Demon Drugs and Social Justice*. Los Angeles: University of California.

Roberts, Les. 2014. "Talkin' Bout My Generation: Popular Music and the Culture of Heritage." *International Journal of Heritage Studies* 20 (3): 262–80.

Sack, Robert. 1983. "Human Territoriality: A Theory." *Annals of the Association of American Geography* 73 (1): 55–74.

Samuel, S. 2012. "I Feel A$AP When He Says He Embraced [Houston] But It's Gotta Be More Than That." *Sohh.com*, February 8, 2012. http://www.sohh.com/i-feel-aap -when-he-says-he-embraced-houston-but-its-gotta-be-more-than-that/.

Sarig, Roni. 2007. *Third Coast: OutKast, Timbaland, and How Hip-Hop Became a Southern Thing*. New York: Da Capo Press.

Shelemay, Kay Kaufman. 2011. "Musical Communities: Rethinking the Collective in Music." *Journal of the American Musicological Society* 64 (2): 349–90. doi:10.1525/ jams.2011.64.2.349.

Shilcutt, Katherine. 2011. "Still Standing." *Houston Press*, January 12, 2001.

Silver, Nate. 2015. "The Most Diverse Cities Are Often the Most Segregated." FiveThirtyEight. May 1, 2015. https://fivethirtyeight.com/features/the-most-diverse-cities -are-often-the-most-segregated/#fn-1.

Sketch the Journalist. 2011. "Von Won Enlists NuWine and Lil Keke for One City under God." *Houston Chronicle*, March 3, 2011.

Stanton, Robert. 2011. "Hip Hop World Mourns Death of Money Clip D." *Houston Chronicle*, November 27, 2011.

———. 2013. "Two Houston Neighborhoods Named the Most Dangerous in America." *Houston Chronicle*, April 30, 2013.

Stefano, Michelle. 2022. *Practical Considerations for Safeguarding Intangible Cultural Heritage*. New York: Routledge.

Styll, John. 1986. "Editor's Note." *CCM Magazine*, February 1986.

Thornton, Sarah. 1996. *Club Cultures: Music, Media, and Subcultural Capital*. Middletown, Conn.: Wesleyan University Press.

Turner, Patricia. 1993. *I Heard It through the Grapevine: Rumor in African-American Culture*. Berkeley: University of California Press.

United States Census Bureau. 2021. "Houston City, Texas; Harris County, Texas; Texas." Quick Facts. https://www.census.gov/quickfacts/fact/table/houstoncity texas,harriscountytexas,TX/PST045221.

Van Igen, Cathy. 2003. "Geographies of Gender, Sexuality, and Race." *International Review for the Sociology of Sport* 38 (2): 201–16.

Waites, Brian. 2012. "Beautiful Noise Alive and Well in Houston." *The Signal*, March 5, 2012. http://uhclthesignal.com/wordpress/2012/03/05/beautiful-noise-alive-and -well-in-houston/. Accessed February 12, 2013.

Walker, Lance Scott. 2013. *Houston Rap*. Los Angeles: Sinecure Books.

Warren, Karen. 2012. "3 Killed, Rapper Hurt in Shooting." *Houston Chronicle*, June 20, 2012. https://www.chron.com/news/houston-texas/slideshow/3-killed-rapper -hurt-in-shooting-44812.php.

Whitfield, Rani. 2008. "Sipping Syrup: Killing Us Softly." Allhiphop.com. April 2, 2008. https://allhiphop.com/uncategorized/sippin-syrup-killing-us-softly/.

Wilkins, Langston Collin. 2016. "Officially Ridin' Swangas: Slab as Tangible and Intangible Cultural Heritage in Houston, Texas." In *The Routledge Companion to Intangible Cultural Heritage*, edited by Michelle Stefano and Peter Davis, 229–39. London: Routledge.

———. 2021. "SouthernplayalisticCADILLACmuzik: OutKast and the Automobility of the Post-Civil Rights South." In *An OutKast Reader: Essays on Race, Gender, and the Postmodern South*. Athens: University of Georgia Press.

Wilson, William Julius. 1997. *When Work Disappears: The World of the New Urban Poor*. New York: Vintage Books.

Wood, Roger. 2003. *Down in Houston: Bayou City Blues*. Austin: University of Texas Press.

Wray, Dianna. 2020. "The 1980s Oil Bust Almost Broke Houston. Almost." *Houstonia Magazine*, June 9, 2020. https://www.houstoniamag.com/news-and-city -life/2020/06/1982-oil-bust-houston.

INTERVIEWS BY THE AUTHOR

Adrian E. (2012, Houston, Texas, in-person)
Andre Barnes (2012, Houston, Texas, in-person)
Big Al (2012, Houston, Texas, in-person)
Big Be (2012, Houston, Texas, in-person)

Big Love (2021, virtual)
China Boy (2013, Houston, Texas, in-person)
Cl'Che (2011, Houston, Texas, in-person)
Corey Paul (2012, Houston, Texas, in-person)
Craig "BBC" Long (2022, virtual)
Daunte (2012, Houston, Texas, in-person)
D-Risha (2011, Houston, Texas, in-person)
Doughbeezy (2011, Houston, Texas, in-person)
Dunta (2012, Houston, Texas, in-person)
EDF (2012, Houston, Texas, in-person)
E.S.G. (2012, Houston, Texas, in-person)
Ganxsta NIP (2012, Houston, Texas, in-person)
Icey Hott (2011, Houston, Texas, in-person)
Justice Allah (2012, Houston, Texas, in-person)
Lil Randy (2012, Houston, Texas, in-person)
Lil Raskull (2012, Houston, Texas, in-person)
Meyagi (2014, phone)
Nasty Nique Roots (2011, Houston, Texas, in-person)
OG Scott (2012, Houston, Texas, in-person)
P Izm the Mack (2013, Houston, Texas, in-person)
Rob Gullatte (2018, Houston, Texas, in-person)
Sketch the Journalist (2012, Houston, Texas, in-person)
That Purple Bastard (2012, Houston, Texas, in-person)
Tre-9 (2012, Houston, Texas, in-person)
Von Won (2012, Houston, Texas, in-person)
Zavey (2012, Prairie View, Texas, in-person)